Ham Hill: Portrait of a Building Stone

Ham Hill:
Portrait of a Building Stone

Richard Durman

Spire Books Ltd
PO Box 2336
Reading RG4 5WJ
www.spirebooks.com

CIP data:
A catalogue record for this book is available
from the British Library
ISBN 1-904965-09-1
ISBN 978-1-904965-09-1

Designed and produced by Geoff Brandwood & John Elliott
Text set in Adobe Bembo

Printed by Alden Group Ltd
Osney Mead
Oxford OX2 0EF

Cover illustration:
Milton Abbas, Dorset: former Abbey, founded 933, rebuilt 14th/15th century (but without a nave); just visible on the left is Joseph Damer's 18th-century mansion (now a school) in Portland Stone, contrasting with the Ham Hill Stone of the Abbey.

Back cover:
St Aldhelm, first bishop of Sherborne (705-9) as featured with harp in the Wingfield Digby Memorial outside Sherborne Abbey (by R. H. Carpenter, 1884); the other figure is St Wulfsin (bishop 992-1001).

Contents

List of Maps & Diagrams

The author and publishers thank the following for kindly giving their consent to the reproduction of the material specified below:

Diagrams   Dr David Jefferson - 1, 2 and 3

Photographic illustrations
© Crown copyright. NMR - pp. 15, 115(R), 118(R), 132 & 135.
Mike Lawrence - Plate 3 & p. 191(both).
Building of Bath Museum - p. 42.
Bill Putnam - p. 91.
The Friends of Sherborne Abbey - p. 116.
Reproduced by permission of English Heritage. NMR - p. 104.
Royal Mail - p. 127(T).
Patrick Cooke - Plate 26.
Dorothy Bark and Museum of South Somerset - p. 149.

Preface

by Lord Ashdown of Norton-sub-Hamdon

I am one of those most fortunate of beings – I live in a Hamstone cottage in the shadow of Ham Hill and my daily joy when I am home is to take pleasure in this most beautiful and remarkable countryside and its wonderful little villages.

This was love at first sight. My wife and I first visited Norton-sub-Hamdon (one of the real glories of the Hamstone mason's art) in 1971 and fell in love with it immediately. A few minutes later we saw our present house and resolved to have no other. When I leave there, it will be feet first.

For us, many things make this paradise. Our friends first and foremost. The village next (in any season, but especially humming with bees around the lavender hedges in summer). And then the countryside and its maze of ancient paths weaving through the fecundity of Somerset, everywhere to be seen, smelt and heard.

And threading in and out of all of this, giving it substance and backdrop and, somehow or other, even the quality of its light, is the glorious honey-coloured stone of Ham Hill. I find bits fashioned by hands from ages past in my garden – and my neighbour has some bits from a Roman column he found in his.

At first sight, this is sandstone. But look closer and you will see you are deceived. It is actually limestone – the tiny sea creatures who died for the mullions of my windows and the arch of my front door, are still easily visible under a magnifying glass. It is their skeletons which give our walls and quoins and the details produced by the unique skills of the Hamstone craftsmen their durability and resistance to weather, so that on our church walls and in our porches you can still see the individual chisel marks from 500 years ago.

This is a magic stone, more beautiful than its brother from the Cotswolds to the north; and more easily worked than its neighbour from Portland to the south. This book tells you a little of its history and its uses. Read it and you will know more. Visit us and see for yourself, and you will understand our passion.

Paddy Ashdown

Introduction

The stone quarried at Ham Hill is one of Britain's most attractive and in many ways most unusual building stones. Builders have valued its qualities for many centuries and the results of their work have survived in abundance. Some of England's best-loved buildings have been built entirely of Ham Hill Stone: Sherborne Abbey, Forde Abbey, Montacute House, Barrington Court, the manor houses of Sandford Orcas and Bingham's Melcombe, as well as the incomparable group of buildings at Brympton d'Evercy. There are many others built predominantly of some other kind of local stone where the composition has been enhanced by the introduction of Ham Hill Stone for the quoins (the cornerstones of the walls), for the 'dressings' (the shaped stone used in door and window surrounds and architectural features such as string courses, plinths and cornices) as well as for sculptural work. The finest examples, perhaps, are some of the Somerset Perpendicular-style churches such as Isle Abbots and Huish Episcopi, in which the gold colour of the Ham Hill Stone is used as a pleasing foil to the pale grey of the walls of the local Blue Lias stone.

The Romans were the first to quarry it on a significant scale and some worked stone from this period has survived despite the wholesale plundering of sites that has occurred. There was a certain amount of Saxon usage but it was the Normans that worked the quarries more extensively to supply stone for their castles and churches. Over the centuries that followed, Ham Hill became a centre of excellence for stonemasonry and carving, contributing to the high quality of church architecture in Somerset in the 15th and early 16th centuries, and to the many fine Tudor and Jacobean mansions and manor houses of the area. During Stuart and Georgian times there were few Hamstone buildings erected that would match the splendour of the earlier 'golden age' but the stone became very fashionable in Victorian and Edwardian times, turning up in some unexpected places. Before the coming of the railways, buildings containing Ham Hill Stone lay, for the most part, within twenty miles or so of Ham

Hill – though there were some interesting exceptions. But thereafter, from about the 1860s onwards, the stone was transported much further afield. So widely, indeed, that it would be impossible to trace all of it; some interesting examples are St Anne's Cathedral, Belfast and three in Devon – Buckfast Abbey, Knightshayes Court and Sidbury Manor. Other good examples of Hamstone usage can be found in London and the Home Counties, Cambridge, Bristol and Plymouth.

The best places to see Ham Hill Stone used in large quantities are, of course, the towns and villages around the Hill itself where it is used as the local building stone. But within just two or three miles its use diminishes as other local stones come to be used from a handier, and therefore cheaper, source. Because a great many of these other local stones also have a gold or yellow hue it is not always easy to distinguish them at first from Ham Hill Stone. But with a little practice the Ham Hill Stone is easily recognised – even if the identity of the local stone remains in doubt – and it starts to become an 'old friend' looking much the same whether used to build a Norman Castle or a Victorian country mansion. The places I would recommend for looking at Ham Hill Stone (if there were time for no others) are Montacute, Martock, Ilminster and Sherborne. And of these Sherborne, though the furthest away from the quarries, really 'has it all', which is why it features in every one of the 'time blocks' that make up the later chapters. Yet, Sherborne's principal building stone is not Ham Hill at all but Sherborne Building Stone. Thus the whole town is full of examples of a phenomenon that occurs again and again – Ham Hill Stone being used where a local stone is not, for some reason, considered good enough, either in appearance or durability. This might just be for the quoins and dressings or for the entire façade of the building depending on its prestige or on what the owner could afford. In Chapter 8 I suggest that the stone is used in this way within a 'sphere of influence' (perhaps as large as 1,000 sq. miles) whose limits are defined by similar areas of other prestigious stones.

The quarries declined in the 20th century but have been re-opened in the last twenty years or so and appear to have a sustainable future, provided sensible decisions are reached on the various 'conservation' issues that are nowadays seen as so important but are so difficult to resolve. Once again the stone is being used both for a great deal of local housing and other development as well as for more prestigious projects in London and elsewhere. Stone tiles are again in production and the making of lime on Ham Hill is another possible future development.

The first chapter is mainly about Ham Hill itself; Chapters 2 - 4 deal with the stone and the quarries; Chapter 5 takes a wider look at the building stones of the region and Chapter 6 is a sort of guided tour of the places closest to Ham Hill in which the stone is used in abundance. Chapters 7 – 12 (and also 14, after an interlude about lime in Chapter 13) range from Roman times to the present day and are divided into time blocks so as to give some sort of chronological sequence and an indication of how and where the stone was being used during each of those periods. I have done this to avoid jumping about between Norman and Georgian, say, but there may be some blurring of the edges between the 'time blocks'. The last chapter looks at some of the issues that are likely to affect the future of the quarries and the stone that they produce.

Any review of stone buildings from early times will inevitably include a large number of churches. Not only was the church often the only building made of stone in a particular settlement but it is usually (not least for that reason) the one that has survived there the longest. It is also the building that is the most accessible. For example, there are many fine country houses that might have qualified for inclusion in this survey but are neither open to the public nor visible from the highway. But a church can always be visited and studied if only (as is increasingly the case today) from the outside – though I am glad to report that perhaps as many as four out of five were open when I visited them.

I have used metric measurements for the most part but have given distances over the ground in miles. I have nothing against kilometres but so long as distances on all our road signs are stated in miles it seems perverse to use anything else. Where an old document refers to shillings and pence or to feet and inches I have assumed that the reader would prefer to see them unadorned and would find 'conversions' an unnecessary irritation.

That invaluable source of reference, *The Buildings of England* series, was created by Sir Nikolaus Pevsner (1902-83) and is still informally referred to as 'Pevsner' (and probably always will be!). However, it has developed into an important institution in its own right and, as more new volumes are published under different editorship, it is becoming less appropriate to refer to it formally in this way. It will be referred to here by the abbreviation '*BoE*'. Similarly, the *Victoria History of the County of Somerset* will be referred to as '*VCH*'. The most important volumes for present purposes are 2 (1911), 3 (1974) and 4 (1978). Volume 2 contains an account of stone extraction in the county at pp. 393-8; volumes 3 and 4 cover parts of 'Hamstone country', although other parts remain to be covered.

There are many people to whom my grateful thanks are due: to the publishing team for all their advice and practical wisdom; to Dr David Jefferson for his invaluable contribution on the formation of Ham Hill Stone; to Richard England of the Ham Hill and Doulting Stone Co. and Mike Lawrence of Ham Hill Stone Co. Ltd who were both generous with their time and patience in giving me the benefit of their experience of the stone business and of Ham Hill Stone in particular; to geologists Hugh Prudden and Jo Thomas; to John Parfit who drew the plans for me; to all those who have so kindly provided valuable historical references and material, Chris Webster (Somerset CC Planning Dept), Claire Pinder (Dorset CC Planning Dept), Stephen Minnitt, (Taunton Museum), Peter

Woodward (Dorset County Museum), John Allan (Royal Albert Museum & Art Gallery, Exeter), Barbara Wood (Museum of South Somerset) as well as Alan Richards (Stoke-sub-Hamdon) and Roman historian, Bill Putnam; to David Bromwich, Somerset Local History Librarian at Taunton, who has been unfailingly helpful; to local authority historic building advisers whom I consulted for 'leads' on Hamstone buildings especially Mark Stobbs, Collette Hall, Richard Bayliss, Patrick Bowes, Chris Pancheri and John Maidment; to other local government officers who have assisted with guidance and information – especially Alison Henry, Andrew Cato, Greg Venn and Katy Menday; to Tom McCaw (Land Agent, Duchy of Cornwall); to John Crook (Archaeologist, Winchester Cathedral); to John Thorpe (Keystone Historic Building Consultants); to Bridget Litchfield and Helen Brown (National Trust Building Surveyors); to Robert Thomas (Plymouth 'informant') and Steve Slatcher (Cambridge 'informant'); to each of the practitioners referred to in the text; to every one of the house owners who have been kind enough to allow me to visit their homes and take photographs. And above all to my wife, Sheila, without whose interest and support this endeavour would have been impossible.

1

Setting the Scene

Ham Hill in south Somerset has the unusual distinction of being both an important prehistoric hillfort and the source of one of the most attractive building stones in England. Quarrying only takes place now at its extremities and the Hill forms part of a country park open to the general public. It is often called Hamdon Hill but if you want to be really pedantic 'Hill' is unnecessary as the suffix 'don' (Old English 'dun') already means hill. So the name should either be simply Hamdon – and this is the form reflected in the names of its two dependent villages, Stoke-sub-Hamdon and Norton-sub-Hamdon – or Ham Hill. The stone is usually called Ham Hill Stone or Hamstone. (An older usage you sometimes come across is 'Hamdon' stone.) I intend to use the term 'Hamstone' for adjectival use ('Hamstone buildings') but to call the stone 'Ham Hill Stone'. Complete consistency is not guaranteed!

Ham Hill stands at the conjunction of the hilly country of south Somerset and west Dorset and the flatlands of the Somerset Levels. On its south side it merges into the surrounding hilly landscape; by contrast, its northern end stands out above the flat land below like the prow of a ship. The obelisk on its northern tip could be a vertical bowsprit. Its defensive qualities are clear and it has an air of pride and impregnability. This may have been justified in prehistoric times, but the Romans not only overcame it but did so with greater ease than they had experienced at Maiden Castle not long before, as they made their way westwards through the country of the Durotriges in the early stages of their occupation of Britain. So Ham Hill is best seen from the north and this is the way anyone seeing it for the first time should approach it. And as it happens this is the way that most people *are* likely to see it for the first time, for just over half a mile away (exactly 1km as it happens) lies the A303 trunk road that takes the bulk of traffic from London and the Home Counties down to the south-west peninsula. The route of the A303 is an interesting one as it passes through Wiltshire and Somerset, and Ham Hill takes its place among several important landmarks. The first is Stonehenge, set in a landscape rich with prehistoric monuments and lying close to the site of Amesbury Abbey, an early foretaste of Celtic and Arthurian legend. But it is King Alfred rather than Arthur who features next in the form of 'Alfred's Tower' the three-sided 18th-century brick tower that dominates the landscape of east Somerset and the Wiltshire borders. It is here, as the modern traffic speeds along on a fine stretch of dual carriageway, that once lay Penselwood, an almost impenetrable barrier of thick forest and scrubby heathland that stretched down to the Dorset coast. By Alfred's time this wilderness was being tamed, but in the early days of the Saxon conquest of England it was an important factor in Somerset not being quelled until long after Hampshire and Wiltshire. So it is no surprise that Somerset, as a seat of British resistance, lays claim both to Avalon and Camelot and it is 'Camelot' that we now see on our left in the form of South Cadbury Castle. It is an impressive Iron Age hillfort, re-fortified by the British after the

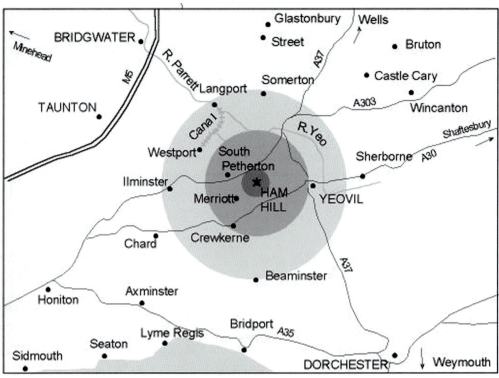

Map 1: Ham Hill location map with the 'Hamstone country' superimposed.

14

legions had left, that stands at the north end of a charming range of hills that runs down to Sherborne and embraces the church and manor house of Sandford Orcas within its folds. The next distinctive sight is St Michael's Hill at Montacute (the *mons acutus* that gives its name to this former ancient borough) rising like a small extinct volcano with a similar hill to its right. St Michael's Hill is topped by an observatory tower in a hilltop clearing but the second hill (Hedgecock Hill) is fully wooded and marks the start of Hedgecock Woods that lead to our destination, Ham Hill. In the meantime we have joined the line of the Fosse Way that ran down from Bath (and beyond) to the Devon coast at Seaton. The Roman engineers steered a cunning course hereabouts, staying clear of the Somerset Levels (a winter flood plain in those times) and of the hills to the south. For here, as at South Cadbury, Ham Hill is an outlier of a series of hills running south to the coast. This cluster of hills in south Somerset is perhaps more like Dorset than Somerset although they have their own distinctive character.

The most dramatic route to the top of Ham Hill is from Stoke-sub-Hamdon that lies hard against its northern side. The road to the top is steep and climbs 75 m from the village to a height above sea level of 130m. From here the views are magnificent both to the north (across the Somerset

Aerial view of the northern spur of Ham Hill from the north-west (in 1997): the prehistoric earthworks, the quarrying taking place at that time, and the remains of older working all stand out clearly.

15

Levels to the Mendip Hills) and towards Wiltshire to the east and towards Devon to the west. There are two other ways of driving to the top of the Hill (in addition to the numerous, more interesting, ways to get there on foot). From Yeovil the country park is signed from the A30 on the west side of the town. This route winds narrowly upwards through Odcombe before flattening out on the plateau of the Hill. A more attractive route lies further west via Little Norton (a 'suburb' of Norton-sub-Hamdon) from which a narrow road rises steeply up the western flank of the Hill through woodland and ferny banks.

The terrain of the Hill itself will come as a pleasant surprise. Much of it is a fairly featureless plateau but its northern and western part consists of a grass-covered 'moonscape' and is much more dramatic. There is something about it of the Barnack 'Hills and Holes' (the disused medieval stone quarries near Peterborough) though the site is unusually elevated and the workings more irregular. The history of quarrying here will be considered in Chapter 4, but as you wander about in acre after acre of disused quarry you feel that the real quarrying that is still taking place is in danger of becoming a sideshow to that history. The industry is alive and well once again, after long periods of inactivity since the last war, but the constraints under which it must operate are formidable (see Chapter 15).

The country park (which is a good deal larger than just Ham Hill) has been imaginatively created and managed by South Somerset District Council. So far as the old quarries are concerned, a balance has had to be struck between providing an exciting environment in which children can play adventurously and people of all ages can explore, and, on the other hand, ensuring that nobody is exposed to undue hazards of the kind you would expect to find in a disused quarrying area. Specific items of interest connected with the industrial heritage of the site are a dramatic quarry face

Ham Hill from the west, showing the war memorial (obelisk on the left), the earthworks defining the northern spur and the houses rising up the side of the Hill from Stoke-sub-Hamdon.

Westward view from Ham Hill over Norton-sub-Hamdon.

(known as 'Deep Quarry') about 30m high and a disused stone limekiln. The site also functions as a nature reserve (though not officially designated as such) with a rich variety of grasses, flowers, insects and birds. The park is sufficiently large and complex in its terrain to contain a permanent orienteering course, the special 'O-map' having been prepared by Quantock Orienteers. It is also an excellent centre for country walks and rambles. The popularity of the park has ensured the continuing operation of the *Prince of Wales* public house in its unusually isolated location in the middle of the Hill.

The old quarrying area is so visually dominant that it is easy to forget at first that you are also standing in one of England's largest hill forts. Indeed it is the largest in England to have been wholly enclosed by man-made earthworks, a distance of about three miles – though not all those earthworks still exist. The fortifications fall into two distinct sections: the shorter section around the northern spur and the longer section around the

Part of the old workings looking north towards the Prince of Wales.

remainder of the fort (see Map 2). They are thought to be from the Iron Age although the northern spur may have been fortified first (possibly with a southern line of defence that has now gone), perhaps as early as the Bronze Age.[1] Flint finds have shown that the Hill has been occupied since the Mesolithic period of the Stone Age (from say 8,000 years ago). It is likely that it was an exceptionally important site to early man. The prominence of the northern spur as a landmark in a region that comprised a series of forests and marshes would have made it a site of great significance and refuge. It is distinctly possible that it contained the same kind of Neolithic 'causewayed enclosure' – more social or religious in

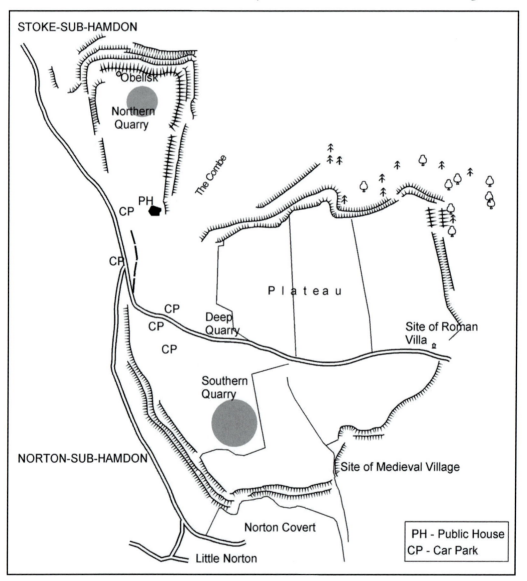

Map 2: Ham Hill - principal features.

function than defensive – that can be found at Whitesheet Hill in Wiltshire and Hembury Hill in Devon. Ham Hill lies roughly midway between these other sites and each of them has its enclosure sited near the end of a prominent hilltop giving wide views over the surrounding country, in other words just like the northern spur.

It has been suggested[2] that the location of Ham Hill was significant in other ways, standing at the point of divide between the hilly country to the south and the flat areas to the north and between the 'highland' zone of western England and the 'lowland' zone of southern and eastern England, giving it a 'central place' role that, certainly by the Iron Age, was demonstrated by its intensive occupation and wealth. Its later earthworks may have been intended more as an indication of prosperity and prestige rather than as a means of defence. With people making journeys to it from different directions, the Hill would also have been on an important cross-country route. The idea of a major road going over the Hill itself would seem to us today as rather peculiar (as it would have done to the Romans) but in a different and more hostile terrain it would have been more natural to seek higher ground. At its northern end the prehistoric route is believed to have been via the field still known as the Combe on the east side of the northern spur rather than the shorter, steeper approach on the west side that is used today. One purpose of the ramparts around the southern section of the camp may have been to enclose and control this important trade route.

The long history of stone quarrying is itself an interesting feature of the site but it has been responsible for destroying many of the remains that archaeologists would otherwise expect to find, especially in the important northern spur. Thus there is no hard evidence of a causewayed enclosure or of a Roman camp, though it is 'inconceivable'[3] that the fort would have been left without a military garrison after its capture. The military role would gradually have declined but the northern spur remained an important focus of Roman occupation including quarrying. We do know, however, that a large villa was built on the 'plateau' sector of the hillfort in the south-east corner, because its site was discovered and first excavated in 1907. A Roman country villa served as a large farmhouse as well as the home of an extended family and its servants and retainers. It is possible that the estate managed from the villa constituted the whole of the hillfort including the quarrying operation.

Excavations have not yet revealed how the Hill may have been used during the Saxon period, though there must have been some quarrying because building elements in which Ham Hill Stone has been used have survived from this period (see Chapter 7). However, it is unlikely that it was ever re-fortified to any great extent, since, when the region was under threat from the Danes in the early years of the 11th century, South Cadbury Castle was re-strengthened as an emergency fort and a temporary mint established there in place of the one at Ilchester.[4] In view of the difficulty of defending Ham Hill from the south, South Cadbury would have been a more natural choice. Similarly, the site chosen by the Norman invaders for their local castle was not Ham Hill but the conical St Michael's Hill at Montacute; the Ham Hill quarries would, however, now be used more intensively as Saxon churches were rebuilt or enlarged and new churches, monasteries and castles were built. As we go on further into the Middle Ages the role of the Hill in the life of the local people becomes more varied. The settlements all around the Hill will generally have become more established and more populous – though one, Witcombe, just outside the south-east corner of the ramparts, had already declined by the early 17th century and was later entirely abandoned. It was no longer necessary for people to live on Ham Hill for reasons of security, though it is quite likely that a former hamlet variously referred to as South Ameldon or Suth Meldon stood on the northern spur and was a quarrying village. Apart from its use for quarrying, the land within the earthworks was now being seen as a communal resource providing land for animals to graze (especially sheep), for wood for fuel and timber, and for the holding of fairs. The existence of a fair is first recorded in 1102 and a charter of 1118 indicated that it extended over thirteen days, although by the 17th century it appears to have been confined to 25 April (St Mark's Day). By then the original trading role of the medieval fair had no doubt largely given way to a recreational one. The fair may well account for the distinct circular area in the north-eastern corner of the spur sometimes called the 'Frying Pan' or the 'Amphitheatre'. It adjoins the (much less distinct) so-called 'equestrian enclosure'. Perhaps the Frying Pan was a sale ring for horses, a kind of early Tattersalls. There were also rabbit warrens, one on the spur and one on the plateau, but these were very much private aristocratic creations rather than being for communal benefit. Another legacy of the fair days was the 'fair house' of which part still exists as a section of the garden wall of the *Prince of Wales*. During the early part of the 19th century the fair had not been held for several years and the fair house was converted to use as a poor house. The Hill continued its function as a cross-country route and in the 18th century comprised part of the London to Exeter coach route. This route also passed through Montacute, which did rather well out of it.

A notable feature of the Hill that has now gone was 'the Ham Stone', a single slab of stone believed to have been about 20 feet high and measuring about 20 feet by 30 feet that stood at the spot where the parishes of Stoke, Norton and Montacute meet. It gives us our first chance to meet Thomas Coryate (1577-1617) from nearby Odcombe, who toured Europe and beyond for the sheer pleasure and adventure of it on a scale that was unprecedented at that time. He wrote about some of his European travels in *Coryate's Crudities* published in 1611. He marvelled at many of the things he saw and described them with great enthusiasm, but he could never

Country Park sign on road from Little Norton, one of a number of inscribed Hamstone signs associated with the Country Park.

forget his origins or lose his pride in his native Ham Hill. Thus in describing a lake in Savoy he writes:

> Yea there are many thousand stones in that lake much bigger than the stones of Stoneage [Stonehenge] by the town of Amesbury in Wilt-shire, or the exceeding great stone upon Hamdon Hill, in Somerset-shire, so famous for the quarre, which is within a mile of the Parish of Odcombe, my dear natalitiall place.[5]

The Ham Stone was sold for building stone in 1824 and was duly broken up.

The immediate locality is one of great charm and interest. This is almost entirely due to its geology. Map 4 (see colour plate 9) shows how it forms part of an area of Yeovil Sands stretching (locally) from Ilminster to Yeovil. Whilst the western part of this zone is mainly flat, the remainder is hilly. The sandy content of these hills has given rise to the distinctive local feature known as the holloway or hollow lane formed by centuries of wear from people, animals and carts. These lanes are usually flanked by strips of woodland and their banks, too, have often been taken over by the local trees and plants. One that thrives especially well is the Hart's Tongue Fern, which could well serve as the emblem of the region. Where the underlying 'rock' of Yeovil Sands is exposed, its surface is often punctuated by nodules of lime-cemented sand known as 'doggers'. These have not worn at the same rate as the surrounding sand and in places can protrude by up to half a metre. The other distinctive feature of the area, of course, is the golden Ham Hill Stone used in so many of the buildings in the surrounding villages and towns, either by itself, where the client could afford it, or alongside other

A local holloway: these sunken lanes are a distinctive feature of those parts of south Somerset and west Dorset where Yeovil Sands and Bridport Sands predominate.

local limestones. The stone was extracted primarily from Ham Hill itself where the beds are thickest, but narrower beds of the same type of rock exist at Chiselborough Hill and Chinnock Hill to the south and, further south again, in high ground near North Perrott. Some quarrying has taken place in the past in these other locations, but never on the same scale as at Ham Hill and probably not for at least two centuries.[6] The villages that ring Ham, Chiselborough and Chinnock Hills are (anti-clockwise from the north end of Ham Hill) Stoke-sub-Hamdon, Norton-sub-Hamdon (with Little Norton), Chiselborough, West Chinnock and Middle Chinnock, East Chinnock, Odcombe and Montacute. Notable 'Hamstone' villages a little further out are Ash, Hinton St George, South Petherton, Shepton Beauchamp, Merriott, Haselbury Plucknett, West Coker, East Coker and Tintinhull. The local towns in which Ham Hill Stone predominates are Martock (though some might call it a large village) and Crewkerne. Many of Yeovil's buildings have made interesting use of Ham Hill Stone but it does not predominate in the same way as in the other places named. This area will be examined more closely in Chapter 6. And there are two other towns that, size for size, have more of the stone than Yeovil, even though they are further away from Ham Hill: Ilminster and Sherborne.

So the beds of Ham Hill Stone have provided great service: they have ensured that the hills on which it can be found have not eroded away and

Contrasting uses of Ham Hill Stone. Left: a cottage in the Somerset village of Coat (near Martock). Right: luxury apartments in London (Hampshire House, Bayswater).

they have allowed the local buildings and settlements to take on an air of distinction. Other local limestones also have a golden warmth about them, but they are not suitable for high-quality ashlar work or fine carving and are considerably enhanced by the use of Ham Hill Stone for quoins and dressings. How these beds of hardwearing stone came to exist where they did will be discussed in the next chapter.

2

The Classification and Formation
of Ham Hill Stone

One day in July 1910 members of the Somerset Archaeological and Natural History Society (SANHS) were conveyed in carriages and motor cars from Yeovil (where they were holding their 62nd Annual Meeting) for an 'excursion' to Ham Hill.[1] They had set themselves a demanding agenda – to call first at Preston Plucknett (see p. 119-20) and then, at Ham Hill, to walk around part of the hillfort and some of the stone quarries and to hear three different papers delivered *en plein air* about various aspects of this unusual place – and all this before lunch! A paper on the geology of the hill was delivered by Rev. H. H. Winwood (Somerset's most distinguished amateur geologist at that time) and he was soon alluding to the great controversy that surrounded the classification of the rock which comprised the Hill, a controversy that he characterised as 'dividing the east from the west'. Despite all this learned attention, given at a time when geology was hardly in its infancy, the conclusions the Society reached that day were different from the views of present-day geologists or, at any rate, were expressed in very different terms from those that would be used today. None of this would matter were it not for the fact that the way that Ham Hill Stone was viewed then has clouded the issue of what it is, and the way it has been written about, ever since. The incident also acts as a warning that there is nothing easy about a proper comprehension of Ham Hill Stone! But rather than pitchfork the reader into the difficult bit, a more gentle step by step approach will be adopted.

Our understanding of the rocks and minerals of which the earth is made is a recent phenomenon. The accepted wisdom in the West, from Classical times and throughout the Middle Ages, had been that all matter consisted of earth, air, fire or water, 'earth' including anything from soil and sand to the hardest rock. It was only in the 17th century that a more 'scientific' approach to observable data was taken, laying the groundwork for the Industrial Revolution and for modern science. Yet the principal fields of scientific learning that benefited from all this were astronomy, biology and technology. Little attention appears to have been given to the earth itself; this would come in the following century. William Smith (1769-1839), who derived his knowledge from his work as a surveyor of canals (and who lived near Bath for much of his life), is often regarded as the father of English geology, being the first to understand and explain stratification. Charles Lyell's *Principles of Geology* was published in 1830, laying the base for modern geological study. Such is the complexity of the subject today that it is more appropriate to talk of the 'geologic sciences' rather than simply 'geology'. For example, anyone wishing to acquire a scientific understanding of building stones would need (at least) to study mineralogy (relating to the minerals of which rocks are composed), sedimentary petrology (concerned with the formation and classification of sedimentary rocks), stratigraphy (to do with the sequence of layers in sedimentary rock), and geomorphology (concerned with the surface processes that create the landscapes of the world). Yet, of course, the men who created the monuments of the Classical age or the medieval masons who built the great cathedrals knew nothing of these geologic sciences. Their choice and use of materials was based on practical wisdom inherited from earlier generations and on their own experience or, at times, from trial and error. Nor is the position really any different today. It is not *necessary* to know when or how a particular type of stone was formed or why it possesses different qualities from another type of stone. All that matters to the designer or builder (apart from its cost) is whether it will do the job expected of it and how it will 'look'.

Is the same true of anyone looking at the completed building? Will your *aesthetic* appreciation be affected by lack of knowledge of the geological history of the materials of which it is made? We are on the edge of murky waters here, because philosophers tell us that visual beauty is not just a matter of line, form, colour, texture and so on but of the spectator's associations and experience. When Sir Christopher Wren built St Paul's Cathedral of Portland Stone he only knew that it was the 'right' stone for the job. For all his advanced scientific knowledge he would have had no way of knowing when and how it was created. So does it matter to us? Well, we are making our study of the building in the 21st century which not only straightaway puts St Paul's in a different historical context from that in which it was seen by Wren's contemporaries, but it means we look at it with the benefit of knowledge gained since Wren's death. Our 'general knowledge' is likely to embrace a broad understanding of how rocks were formed millions of years ago when the world was very different. We may indeed wish to know more about the nature and formation of Portland Stone. The danger is that that curiosity becomes a distraction: that we study

St Paul's from a distance of a few inches with a lens in our hand and do not stand back and look at it as a building. But to ignore altogether *why* Portland Stone has the qualities it does is surely to miss out on an important aspect of an appreciation of the building.

It pays to creep up on Ham Hill Stone in easy stages. This way we can try to find out what it *is* by establishing what it is not and by eliminating other categories of rock as we go along. (The term 'rock' is used here for what is in the ground, in the objective sense used by a geologist dispassionately studying what it consists of. 'Stone' is the commodity extracted from the rock by people for their human requirements.) The world's rocks are commonly classified as being igneous, sedimentary or metamorphic. Igneous rocks are those that have been solidified from a molten state, ranging from rock that has cooled slowly deep within the earth's crust ('intrusive') to rock formed from the lava and dust spewed out by volcanoes ('extrusive'). If you wish to see granite used as the local building material you would need to go, for example, to Dartmoor or Cornwall or, in the north of the country, Cumbria or Northumbria. Its proverbial hardness makes it virtually indestructible but also makes it very difficult to shape or carve. It must have taken a special breed of stonemason to achieve even the rudimentary crockets and finials that we find on the churches of Cornwall and Dartmoor.

Metamorphic rock is a pre-existing rock, either igneous or sedimentary, that has been altered as a result of colossal forces brought to bear on it by intense heat or pressure. Some of the world's most interesting and attractive stone, such as the many different types of marble, are metamorphic but in England only slate comes into this category. (England has several varieties of stone that have been given the name 'marble' but none of it is a true, metamorphic, marble.) Nature has been very kind in the case of slate because the forces that caused it to be so hard have also allowed it to be easily split. Slates for roofing in many parts of England have traditionally come from North Wales (nowadays more often than not it comes from Spain) but Somerset once had its own slate quarries – in the southern part of Exmoor around Treborough and Wiveliscombe. The quality of the slates produced was not quite up to that of Welsh slates but they were a valuable resource while they lasted and were used, for example, at Dunster Castle in 1426.[2]

Ham Hill Stone is a *sedimentary* rock – as is 70% of the rock that covers the earth's surface. In England, there is so little rock that is *not* sedimentary that if it were concentrated in one area it would cover roughly the area of Cornwall. It is not very surprising that there is so much sedimentary rock because it derives from the other two categories, igneous and (to a lesser extent) metamorphic, as well as from the remains of living creatures, and after about $4^{1}/_{2}$ billion years the earth has had time to mature and to make it in abundance. While the entire surface of the earth was erupting and heaving there was no opportunity for sedimentary rocks to be formed, but after a crust had developed and water had appeared it would not be long, against the vast time-scale of the earth's history, before the process of erosion would commence and a new form of rock created that we call sedimentary.

Sedimentary rock, as its name implies, starts its life in the seas, oceans and rivers. It is formed both from the breaking down of other rock into small particles by the action of water and weather, and also by the build up of the remains of living creatures in the sea (or river estuary). In either case these new particles undergo *lithification*, that is to say new rock is created as a result of physical and chemical processes taking place over millions of years. And, of course, these processes are taking place *now* as the rocks of the future are being slowly, very slowly, formed. The fact that we find these rocks on dry land indicates that their initial formation is only one part of their history. Subsequent upheavals of the earth's surface have caused them to be found where we see them today often at a great height and far from the sea. One – not very surprising – principle of sedimentary petrology (though nobody had worked it out until William Smith came along) is that younger layers (or strata) of rock are found above older ones. But this idea becomes useful where the forces pushing up the rock have also caused it to fold, sometimes leaving an older layer at a higher level than a younger one. The 'correct' order of the levels can be read by following another principle, namely that the strata of rock can be traced for long distances through a landscape.

It is difficult to grasp that a great deal of what we call 'rock' originated from organic material. However, a useful example of the processes involved can be found in many back gardens. Anyone who maintains a compost heap will know that in less than a year a heap of organic material will shrink to about half its size, become quite dense and solid and change its colour to a dark brown. It will also appear stratified, the different 'strata' corresponding to the layers of material laid one on top of another as the heap is gradually built up. It is easy to imagine that in 'only' a few thousand years the heap would become extremely dense and almost black and that if it were underground it would, with the greater pressure it would be under, eventually become the category of rock that we call coal. The degree of compression in sedimentary rock will depend on the weight of higher layers which is why, as we shall see, the best building stone is often found towards the base of the band (or 'horizon'). The greater wonder, perhaps, is not that rock can be formed from living creatures but that traces of those creatures can be found in the form of fossils millions of years after their death.

We can narrow the description of Ham Hill Stone down further by describing it as a limestone. This tells us that it consists *primarily* of the remains of sea creatures, either their skeletons or their shells or both. The variety of life in the waters of the earth has meant that there are many varieties of limestone ranging from chalk to harder types such as Portland Stone or, indeed, Ham Hill Stone. The other category of sedimentary rock is sandstone made up from particles worn or washed away from other rocks. The colour and texture of sandstones can vary considerably – from soft sandy yellow material (such as Yeovil Sands), through somewhat harder greensands to very dense and hard-wearing stones including Devonian Sandstone that can be found right across Exmoor for example. Sandstones are generally more homogeneous in their make–up than limestone.

It is sometimes a matter of degree, and therefore a matter of personal opinion, as to whether a particular sedimentary stone is a sandstone or a limestone. One person's 'limey sandstone' might be another's 'sandy limestone'. (We shall see a good example of this in relation to Salcombe Regis Stone – see p. 44.) After all, it would be too much to expect the degraded and washed-away particles of rock (the potential sandstone) when they reach the sea to remain neatly separated from the accumulations of shells and other organic material (slowly turning into limestone).

So far, the terms that geologists use to indicate the *age* of rocks have been avoided, because for present purposes they are an unnecessary complication. More will be said about them in later chapters, but there is one that cannot be avoided here because it refers to the category in which Ham Hill Stone has been put by geologists, and that term is Jurassic. The general geological pattern of England is that the younger rocks are in the South-East – 'rocks' here seems a misnomer since we are talking largely of chalk and clay – and the older ones in the west and north. Running down through the middle of the country, from the Yorkshire coast near Scarborough to the coast of Dorset, is a band of rocks that is predominantly limestone and is of 'middling age' (formed about 150 to 200 million years ago) called Jurassic. Now, in the South-East good building stone is hard to come by; there are some good quality sandstones to be had in Kent and Surrey but for the most part deposits consist of chalk and a variety of clays. There are some fine building stones to be found to the north-east of the Jurassic band but at the same time there are many that are either too hard, lack durability or are not very attractive. On the other hand, the Jurassic band yields building stones that are some of the most distinctive and attractive in the country. They have given us the grey-gold villages of the Cotswolds and of Northamptonshire, the cream-coloured terraces of Bath as well as the sparkling grey stone, shipped round the coast from Portland, used in so many of London's major buildings. And it has given us the golden Ham Hill Stone and the wealth of delightful buildings that we shall be looking at in more detail.

So Ham Hill Stone is sedimentary, and is a Jurassic limestone. But there is one more step to take before we can say we have a complete definition; it is an important step because we are now closing in on what makes Ham

Hill Stone very unusual. Many Jurassic limestones are 'oolitic', deriving their name from the fact that the rock is composed primarily of ooliths, spherical grains no more than 1mm across and held together by a 'glue' of calcite. Each type of stone has its own peculiar mix of constituent elements and chemical composition but one of the best examples of a 'pure' oolite is Ketton Stone in Northamptonshire. Portland Stone and Bath Stone are also oolitic, though the latter is often categorised as 'shelly oolitic' with its higher shell content. But Ham Hill Stone is composed almost entirely of shells; it is most certainly not oolitic. John Allen Howe (the only geologist who has ever written a wide-ranging account of the building stones of Britain and beyond) described it as a 'shell' limestone.[3] One term that is often applied to it (to distinguish it from oolitic) is 'bioclastic', that is to say, consisting of broken shelly fragments. Howe reminds us that the processes that led to the formation of shelly limestone are taking place today:

> At certain spots on the British shores – but better examples are found elsewhere – great quantities of marine shells are thrown up by the sea, forming masses of loose shell sand; here and there in these banks the superficial waters have dissolved portions of the carbonate of lime from adjacent parts of the mass, and have redeposited it in patches among the shell-fragments, forming thereby cemented blocks of coherent rock. The same process may be observed going on amid the oyster banks and other shelly areas on the floor of the surrounding seas.[4]

We can at last give Ham Hill Stone a label; it is a bioclastic Jurassic limestone. The difficulties encountered by the learned Somerset gentlemen at Ham Hill in 1910 stemmed from the fact that the sub-division of Jurassic at that time was into two 'series' – Lias and Oolite. This was *entirely a matter of age*, Oolite being the younger of the two. The fossil evidence seemed to show that Ham Hill Stone was part of the Oolite series (though this was a matter of dispute then and is now regarded as incorrect) and it was categorised accordingly. This approach was accepted by the 1910 meeting. Since then, a different approach has been taken to the analysis of limestone that takes account of its appearance and make-up rather than its age (hence the oolitic/bioclastic distinction). Ham Hill Stone is clearly not oolitic by such criteria but unfortunately the description stuck. If it was good enough for geologists to call it oolitic then it would have seemed the safe thing for laymen to do the same and to go on repeating what had once been said. It may be many years before descriptions of Ham Hill Stone as 'oolitic' finally disappear from guidebooks to the area or to individual local buildings.

This begs the question of what *is* the correct current 'stratigraphical' description (i.e. relating to age) of Ham Hill Stone within the general age description of Jurassic – which is divided into Upper, Middle and Lower Jurassic. The answer is 'Lower', but just to make things more complicated the Lower series is still called Lias, which is also a sedimentological term relating to composition. It is said to derive from the name given by West Country quarrymen to the rock consisting of alternate layers of clay and limestone widely found in that region, especially in Somerset where 'layers' would be pronounced 'lias'. Because Lias (more particularly, the building stones called Blue Lias) predominates in the Lower Jurassic group, its name has been attached to, the group. But it is too smooth and dull in appearance to have anything in common with Ham Hill Stone and it is most confusing that the latter is still categorised as Lias. The category is in turn divided into Upper, Middle and Lower Lias and Ham Hill Stone falls into the Upper category — i.e. just below the one that used to be called Oolite but is now called Middle Jurassic. (And, as a further complication, the term 'Inferior Oolite' is still used in relation to certain Middle Jurassic stones. Indeed, they are an important feature of the Ham Hill area and we shall encounter them both in this and later chapters.) Hence, so far as Ham Hill Stone is concerned, *it is best simply to call it 'Jurassic', ignoring the stratigraphical subtleties.*

This just leaves the question of how it may have been formed. From its appearance geologists can deduce that it was formed in shallow water. Rock formed in deep water is generally of an even consistency as the process of the skeletons of sea creatures (and other material) building up over millions of years takes place in a relatively undisturbed fashion. Portland Stone is a supreme example of one that owes its consistency and homogeneity to such a geological history. But shallower water is likely to be subject to constant and irregular movement. There is also likely to be a greater mix of different materials being carried along and deposited, again in an uneven and unpredictable way. Thus Ham Hill Stone consists of shelly material and the remains of a variety of sea creatures but it also contains a great deal of lithified silt and clay. As conditions constantly changed, all these constituents have been mixed up in an infinitely variable

'Current bedding' in Hamstone blocks at Lloyds TSB bank, Salisbury, Wiltshire, characteristic of shallow-water formation.

way. There was also iron present since it makes up 14% of the content of Ham Hill Stone (including some aluminium). There is also more silica present (5%) than in other limestones and it is this that helps bind the various particles together. Ham Hill Stone also contains veins of calcite, running roughly at right angles to the natural bedding plane. These were probably formed at a late stage in the lithification process as splits occurred in the material and the calcite was washed into the cracks. Another

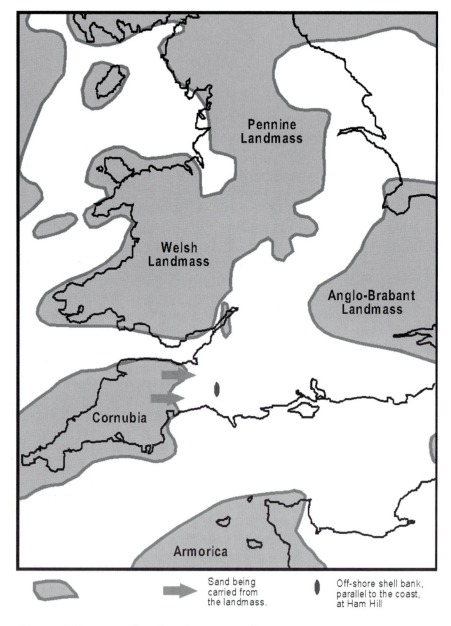

Diagram 1. Formation of Sand Bank at Ham Hill.

consequence of the constant and irregular movement of the water is that it led to the fragments being deposited at different angles. This is called 'current–bedding' or 'cross-bedding' and is characteristic of shallow-water formations and an important aspect of the appearance of Ham Hill Stone.

So what has happened to lead to what we find today? How does an isolated mass of limestone come to be found perched up on top of 'a heap of sand'? Consultant geologist Dr David Jefferson has been advising on stone deposits at Ham Hill for some years and has established a clear and convincing theory of what has taken place.[5] He explains that you have to imagine the area as once occupied by a shallow sea with a relatively flat base and lying between its two nearest landmasses, Cornubia to the west, equivalent to Devon and Cornwall, and Armorica to the south, which extended south-west from Normandy (Diagram 1).[6] Towards the end of what is called the Toarcian Stage of the Lower Jurassic (round about 180 million years ago), gentle warping and uplift of the land resulted in more sandy sediment coming into the area from these adjacent landmasses and forming a large sand bar, now comprising the Yeovil Sands. The relative levels of land and sea kept changing and Jefferson believes that this large sand bar became exposed at least once. In the Ham Hill area, it dried out and became lithified, at least in part, and then broke up to form what is now a layer of conglomerate found at the base of the limestone on Ham Hill. ('Conglomerate' is a form of sandstone containing rounded blocks, pebbles or boulders. Chesil Bank, near Weymouth and Portland, is a potential conglomerate.)

'The shallow water over this submerged island', explains Dr Jefferson,

> became colonised with organisms such as bivalves, brachiopods, bryozoa, cephalopods, corals and crinoids. Currents from the southwest tended to mound the dead shell material into submarine banks. From time to time storms brought sand into the carbonate reef-like environment. At other times the area occupied by the bivalves, corals and other organisms shrunk and sand was deposited. This sand was, of course, being deposited in the sea around the Ham Hill reef-like body at the same time as the shelly limestone was being deposited in this area. These influxes of sand formed the discontinuous beds of sand found today in the limestone. It is possible that sand eventually overwhelmed much of the 'reef'. However, as the surrounding landmasses were eroded away, the supply of sand decreased and calcareous organisms flourished over the whole area forming, what is now, the Inferior Oolite limestone.

These processes are shown in Diagram 2 concluding with a situation that is now hard to visualise, namely a layer of calcareous rock (Inferior Oolite) formed on the bottom of shallow water *above* the level of Ham Hill. Diagram 3 attempts to show what transpired later in the vicinity of Ham Hill including the erosion of the Inferior Oolite. The present distribution of the Ham Hill Stone, believes Jefferson, is due to faulting. The whole area is broken up by a series of faults and joints. The blocks of ground between these have moved up or down relative to each other. The ground at the south end of Ham Hill has dropped relative to the north end. As erosion has levelled off the top of the Hill, this has resulted in more limestone remaining at the south end than the north. Between Ham Hill and Chiselborough Hill the ground has moved up relative to that at these two locations. As a result, the erosion down to the level of the top of Ham Hill has completely removed the limestone from the intervening area. This has exposed the underlying sand, which has then rapidly been weathered away to leave a valley.

The Ham Hill Stone extended from at least the north end of Ham Hill down to North Perrott in the south. Whereas a maximum thickness of 27 m has been quoted in geological studies for Ham Hill, the limestone reaches a maximum of about 6 metres on Chinnock Hill. (Whether this thickness was once greater is not known, since it is not possible to determine how much has been eroded away.) This would fit in with currents from the south-west sweeping across the reef and piling the detritus up in submarine dunes (now the blockstone) in the area of Ham Hill itself.

There is an alternative theory that the limestone was formed in a tidal channel cutting through a sand bar.[7] However, Dr Jefferson points out that the proponents of the theory do not give any source for the shell debris, nor do they account for the largely unbroken nature of the shells, or of the quantity of iron mineral found in the deposit. The last mentioned phenomenon is accounted for on the bank or reef hypothesis, Jefferson believes, by the breakdown of the organic matter trapped in the shell and other debris; this would not be present in shells washed into a channel.

More will be said about the geology of the region and its other building stones in Chapter 5 and, in particular, Map 4 (in colour plate 9) shows the areas of Ham Hill Stone resulting from the processes described above, in the context of the local geology.

3

Qualities as a Building Stone

This chapter examines the qualities or characteristics of Ham Hill Stone that set it apart from others. To assess any building stone it is necessary to consider its *colour* and *texture* and (in many situations) its '*carvability*'. It needs to be 'strong' of course, able to withstand pressure without suffering damage, but for ordinary building purposes – that is to say ignoring sea walls and military defences and other special situations – one stone is usually as good as another. But more importantly, however strong stone may appear to be, it must in the long term be able to withstand the weather and atmosphere; there is no point in building in a particular stone if it is going to give constant problems in the future. This is its *durability*. The number of potential hazards that limestone can run is surprisingly high: for example, damage from frost, salt crystallisation, efflorescence, rainwater, air pollution, 'bio-deterioration' (from algae, lichen, mosses and other growth) and vibration.

Ham Hill Stone's unusual formation (discussed in the previous chapter) has left it with some unusual characteristics, notably, its shelly composition, its high iron content and the frequent presence of bands of clayey material. The high iron content has helped to give the stone its distinctive colour and (with the silica) its proven strength – allowing it to be used in at least three Norman castles. As for its colour, it has been variously described as 'buff', 'ochre', 'brown', 'golden', 'golden-brown', 'golden-grey', 'old gold', 'yellow', 'honey-coloured', 'honey-brown', 'orange-brown' and even 'apricot', 'rosy yellow' and 'raw siena'. This is as much a reflection on the varied nature of the stone as on different personal perceptions. The adjective most frequently used to describe it is 'warm'. Another visual feature is the occasional presence of 'vents', which have allowed oxygen to enter the stone and turn the edges of the vent purple.

The traditional view is that Ham Hill Stone comes in two types – yellow and grey of which the grey is the stronger and more durable. A stone for carving or working, and this is how it is ordered and supplied. Practitioners like Sabran would say that Hamstone is Hamstone wherever it comes from and whenever it was quarried, and that too much can be made of these old distinctions.

The clay bands (which can be anything in width from a few millimetres to 4 or 5 centimetres) by no means appear in all samples (and hardly at all in the Bottom bed); nor do they render the stone unusable where they do appear. It only means that care should be taken as to where that particular sample is used. If it is exposed to the weather, especially a combination of wind and rain or to regular frosts, the clay will soften and loosen and eventually start to fall out, though the whole process might take as much as a hundred years.[5] So the builder of today needs to take a certain amount of care when using Ham Hill Stone to avoid long-term problems. (Chapter 15 covers the wider topic of maintenance and contains examples of this particular form of deterioration and how it has been dealt with.) However, the past is the best indication of the future and the historical survey in later chapters of how Ham Hill Stone has been used provides sufficient evidence that, in general, it will withstand the weather as well as almost any oolitic limestone.

This is backed up scientifically in relation to two critical factors of durability: porosity and resistance to chemical change. Limestone is full of tiny holes, or 'pores', which are liable to soak up rainwater. In serious cases this can lead to internal dampness, as the Bath architect John Wood the Elder (1704-54) discovered in relation to Bath Stone before he began to use thicker facing blocks in exposed positions. But the more pervasive problem is that of the water being absorbed by the limestone and then being affected by frost or by salt crystallisation, in either case leading to damage to the surface of the stone. Most Jurassic building stones have a porosity factor in the range 10% to 30%. Ham Hill Stone has a porosity factor of between 13% and 18%. And it 'scores' even higher in another relevant aspect. Small pores are likely to give more trouble than larger ones because they have a 'sucking' effect (especially micropores less than 0.005mm in diameter) and hold the water more firmly through surface tension. In the case of most Jurassic limestones about 50% to 90% of their pores are micropores but the relevant figure for Ham Hill Stone is 40%. Further tests and analysis have been undertaken on a wide range of building stones in relation to the effect on the stone of the water that has been absorbed.[6] It is not the water by itself that is necessarily the problem but the extent to which the soluble salts it contains crystallise within the stone. Tests undertaken on behalf of the Building Research Establishment (BRE) in 1983 graded 40 different limestones on a scale of from A (the most durable) to F (the least durable). Samples of Ham Hill Stone were graded A to B compared, for example, with Bath Stone (C to F), Portland (C to E) and Doulting (B to D). Yet the BRE would be the first to say that such tests must be treated with caution on account of the way different samples of the same stone can vary so much; 'Hitting with a crowbar is still the best durability test to see if it 'rings true' and is thus free from fissures.'[7] And there is often another threat to durability waiting around the corner.

The characteristic that is perhaps the most commonly attributed to high quality Jurassic limestone is that it is a 'freestone', one that can be readily carved in any direction. A fuller definition (from *A Dictionary of Building* published by Penguin Books) is 'Building stone which is fine-grained and uniform enough to be worked in any direction and can thus be carved. Freestones are generally limestones or fine-grained sandstones.'

'Freestone' is not a scientific term but one that has long been used by stonemasons and others associated with the stone industry. Portland Stone is the classic example of a building stone that lends itself to intricate carving yet remains strong and hard. Bath is another though not so hard or strong as Portland. Thus the stonemasons who worked on St Paul's Cathedral in London or, a little later, on the Circus or the Royal Crescent at Bath could rely on stone that would allow them to carve all the necessary detail time and time again and in accordance with the requirements of the architect or head mason. Can the same be said of Ham Hill Stone? Well, there are certainly many church monuments and other pieces of intricate carving that might lead you to believe so. And it has been described as freestone again and again.[8] The justification, perhaps, for doing so is that in many buildings – indeed in a huge number in the 'region' considered in Chapter 5 (that covers other building stones) – a cheaply available local stone is used for the walls but a superior stone from further afield is used for the quoins and dressings. This finer stone is often called 'freestone' to distinguish it from the local stone and on account of its ability to be shaped or carved or given a smooth finish in a way that is not possible with the local stone. Thus the term freestone tends to be attached in this sense to Ham Hill Stone as

well as to Doulting, Bath or Portland. But when judged against the definition above, Ham Hill Stone cannot truly be said to be a freestone. Stonemasons would not regard it as such and, interestingly, neither quarry company at Ham Hill, nor any other stone merchant that has been consulted, claim that what they supply is 'freestone'. It is too layered and too

Part of the face of Deep Quarry, Ham Hill, showing the naturally fractured nature of the beds as well as tool marks on the stone.

41

patching has done nothing to improve the cathedral's external appearance, which is a tragedy for a building that might otherwise have been one of England's finest. As a local stone for the villages around Lichfield it is attractive enough; it is just that it has not proved an appropriate material for a great cathedral. How much more fortunate were the builders of Lincoln, Wells or Salisbury Cathedrals; all these lie close to the Jurassic limestone belt and all use good quality oolite of different shades – a creamy-brown at Lincoln (where an impressive range of Lincolnshire limestones was available), a creamy-grey at Wells (Doulting Stone) and a grey sandier version of Portland Stone for Salisbury.[12] Bath Abbey (itself a cathedral in Norman times) owes a great deal of its refined charm to the Bath Stone of which it is made. Apart from the matter of colour, it would simply be impossible to create its vaults and tracery in, say, the granite of Dartmoor or the Old Red Sandstone of Exmoor and the Quantock Hills – although the use of a softer limestone has its own problems of durability when used for the exterior of a building.

Exeter Cathedral, too, has benefited from being within ready reach of a plentiful supply of attractive limestone, though, in this instance, water transport has played a key part. The builders relied on a certain amount of local stone but obtained supplies of limestone by sea from Portland and Purbeck and, in greatest quantities, from Beer (not far from Seaton in south-east Devon) as well as from quarries a few miles to the west of Beer at Salcombe Regis (not to be confused with the better known Salcombe in south Devon). Salcombe Stone is actually more often referred to as a sandstone in view of its high sandy content.[13] None of the quarries are far from the sea and the stone was transported to Exeter along the coast to Topsham and the river Exe. Beer Stone is much younger than Jurassic limestone and is, in effect, a hardwearing form of chalk. It would be wrong to regard this area of south-east Devon chalk limestone as forming part of the Jurassic limestone belt, but it is close enough to be regarded as sharing its characteristics rather than those of the rest of Devon. In any event, it was an inspired choice, allowing Exeter to be placed in the category of cathedrals blessed with an appropriate supply of stone. Some stone also came from Caen in Normandy. First introduced by the Normans, Caen Stone has been used in a great many English buildings (Canterbury and Norwich Cathedrals are perhaps the most notable), demonstrating that the overland haulage of stone from more than a few miles away was always avoided if it could be transported by sea or river. Exeter Cathedral even contains some Ham Hill Stone but the quantities were so small that it was transported overland. In any case, Ham Hill is a great deal further from the sea than the other quarries that were used.

This digression into the relative merits of English cathedrals is to show how some building materials can be claimed to enhance the overall effect of a building and some do not. So far as Ham Hill Stone is concerned, it is possible to find examples of where its use has not been appropriate and where another stone might have been used to greater advantage. But such examples are not likely to be found within the area around Ham Hill where it is the predominant building material or in a building built before about 1840. No observer of English buildings will find this surprising. It is simply a natural consequence of the traditions of both vernacular and 'formal' architecture up to that time and of the enormous social upheavals that would occur during the 19th century. Until the coming of the railways and the wider use of mass production most local buildings were built of local materials. There had always been exceptions of course. The builders of royal palaces and castles, of fortified manor houses or of the more important religious buildings would seek stone and timber from far afield if local supplies were inadequate or of unsuitable quality. It was worth paying more for prestige and status. Thus the castle at Castle Cary was partly built in Ham Hill Stone despite the availability of local Inferior Oolite and Blue Lias. The high additional cost of transporting stone fifteen miles or so from Ham Hill was considered to be justified. When the Abbot of Sherborne rebuilt his Salisbury residence in the cathedral close in the 15th century he saw fit to use Ham Hill Stone for the dressings and for the finely carved east porch. But leaving aside these special cases, the buildings of a locality were made of local materials.

Where there was no ready supply of stone the standard material would be timber, the frame being filled in with wattle and daub and the building normally covered in thatch. From the first quarter of the 17th century (earlier in some areas) it became more common to build in brick. According to local practices, the brick would either substantially replace timber-framing or be used as a sturdier in–fill material – often mixed with flint in the chalk areas of the country. That a lack of stone need not be a disadvantage is demonstrated by the charm (and longevity) of the 'timber' villages of Herefordshire or Suffolk or the 'brick and flint' villages of the South Downs or the Chilterns. Nevertheless where stone was plentiful it tended to be used for all manner of local buildings and it is this that lends a pleasing unity to the appearance of settlements or clusters of buildings that have been built of the same stone. This unity is given added force where a consistency of style or scale has been applied, perhaps over several centuries. There is often a sense that the very stones are part of the landscape from which they have come. The two are in harmony, as if the buildings have grown organically out of the land. This can be felt as strongly in the grey granite settlements of Cornwall or in the brown sandstone country of Yorkshire as in the beauty spots of the Cotswolds. However, it is probably the last of these (the pick of the Cotswold villages) that are the best known and the best loved. Their special advantage lies in the particular creamy-grey colour of the oolitic limestone (teetering between warmth and coolness) and the integrity of the roofs with the rest of the buildings.

sub-industry was the burning and slaking of lime for the production of lime mortar, that magical substance to which all well-built buildings owed a great part of their success (see Chapter 13). Lime mortar is undergoing a revival but the old limekiln that can be found in the country park on Ham Hill is now only an interesting relic of industrial archaeology.

With its wealth from the wool trade, Somerset was experiencing a building boom in the 15th century and these may have been Ham Hill's greatest days, regarded not only as the source of a high quality building stone but as a centre of excellence for stonemasonry. For the processes of winning the stone and of preparing it for the building site were seen as two sides of the same coin and a mason would learn both aspects of the trade. Indeed, in the Middle Ages quarries were the usual place where a mason would first learn his trade. One practical reason for ensuring that as much carving as possible was undertaken at the quarry was that it was cheaper to transport blocks of stone that had already been at least rough-hewn to the shape that would be required on site than blocks that were freshly quarried. On the other hand, finely carved stonework would be liable to damage when it was transported by cart. So there would need to be some judgment exercised as to how skills and labour were divided between the quarry and the building site: how far, for example, the craftsmen on site merely fitted together pieces of stone that others had already carved, or the extent to which the majority of the carving was undertaken on site. Perhaps this balance would vary from job to job or even vary as a job progressed according to the men available and the nature of the masonry required at various stages. It is reasonable to assume that such a breadth of expertise, both technical and organisational, had been developed at Ham Hill by the late Middle Ages that the client would turn to 'Ham Hill' for all the building services he required – a sort of 'design and build' package. There is certainly evidence for this approach in the following century, as we shall see in Chapter 10.

The more skilled masons would progress to statuary and other carved details, and those who showed talent as a draughtsman or the broader vision required to design a building would be trained as master masons. Masons were in great demand at this period and would often be sought from far afield. There was often difficulty in obtaining enough masons locally for royal works and there developed a system of effectively press-ganging masons from other parts of the country. In times when men were usually known by their place of origin ('John of X') it is interesting to learn that masons called Norton and Stoke could be found on the rolls of employees (both masons and quarriers) at Vale Royal Abbey,[12] Beaumaris Castle and Caernarvon Castle.[13] One of the most distinguished master masons we know by name from the 14th century was Henry de Yevele (d.1400) who in 1360 became the King's mason for the works at Westminster and the Tower of London. It is possible that 'Yevele' is a rendering of Yeovil; could it have been time spent at the Ham Hill quarries that set him on his great career?

It has been suggested that quarrymen belonged to the same guild, trade society or fraternity,[14] but this may be an extrapolation into the Middle Ages of Thomas Gerard's observations, in 1633, on the system of self-regulation that applied at that time among the masons.[15] Ham Hill might well have been a worthy exception but a leading study of medieval masonry found that there was little evidence (in the country generally) of masons' guilds or of formal apprenticeships in the Middle Ages. Training was normally undertaken in the quarries or within a mason's family or household.[16]

Ham Hill's reputation was evidently as high in the 16th century as it had been in the 15th, John Leland speaking of it in glowing terms when he included Stoke-sub-Hamdon in his investigative 'itinerary' for Henry VIII in 1542: 'Also nearby, at Hamdon, is the famous stone quarry, from which for a long time stone has been taken for all the high quality buildings in the entire region.'[17]

But drastic changes were around the corner as Leland's master turned the life of England upside down. For Ham Hill, the bottom would fall out of the lucrative church and monastery business but there would be compensations during the Tudor and Stuart ages in the form of great houses for the new landed classes – above all nearby Montacute House (completed c.1601) that, for about ten years, would, perhaps, take virtually all the stone the Hill could produce. When Thomas Gerard wrote about the quarries in 1633, he noted the large number of buildings on the Hill, making the quarries 'seeme rather little parishes than quarryes'.[18]

By the early 17th century the quarries in Stoke had largely given way to those in Norton,[19] though four quarries were seen on the spur in the 18th century by the Somerset historian John Collinson[20] and it was at this time that a small settlement appears to have existed on the spur. Much of Stoke had long been in royal ownership and by the 16th century had become part of the possessions of the Duchy of Cornwall (which still has a substantial landholding in the area including the northern spur of the Hill and Hedgecock Woods). The Prince of Wales was Lord of the Manor of Stoke until 1936 when the Lordship and some tracts of land were acquired by Mrs W. F. Quantock Shuldham.

The Phelips family first came to live in Montacute late in the 15th century and Edward Phelips built Montacute House a century later. By the 18th century, if not before, the Phelips family began to take on interests in the Hill including quarrying and the fair. The rights to the fair were leased to Edward Phelips[21] in 1735 and the Duchy had leased four quarries (presumably the four seen by Collinson) to Phelips. The lease was granted in 1739 but in 1727 a petition had been addressed to the Prince of Wales asserting that there were 'four or more ancient quarries on Hambden Hill' great days of this stone lie in the Middle Ages when the quarries were owned by Glastonbury Abbey. The Abbey itself was probably the largest in England and used Doulting Stone on a very large scale. The result of this was that the site of the Abbey became a huge quarry after it was dissolved and much of the stone became used again in Glastonbury and beyond. The Abbey's ownership and control of the quarries was a matter of vexation to the Dean and Chapter of Wells Cathedral during the construction of the present cathedral (c.1180 to c.1430), though the Cathedral did eventually manage to secure a lease of one quarry. At the times when Doulting was unavailable, Chilcote Conglomerate,[3] quarried near Croscombe, proved an adequate substitute. Doulting's high quality as a freestone is vividly illustrated by the carved capitals of Wells Cathedral, one of the greatest collections of medieval carved figures and foliage anywhere in the country. Its wearing qualities may not match those of Portland Stone but at its best – and there is much variety in the beds – they are better than those of Bath Stone. It is widely used in its own local area of Somerset but in the 19th century a railway line came up to the 'back door' of the quarries at Cranmore, which is still the home of the East Somerset Railway now operated by rail enthusiasts. Until the 1930s Doulting Stone was carried by rail to other parts of the country. Buildings in which it has been used are Lancing College in Sussex (though not the chapel), the Cathedral of Bury St Edmunds and Guildford Cathedral.

Dundry was another high quality oolitic freestone that was extensively quarried in medieval times in north Somerset south of Bristol. It can be seen to good effect in Wrington where the soaring church tower is one of the most elegant in Somerset. It was used a great deal in Bristol (including St Mary Redcliffe) and within the see of Bath and Wells, the bishop owning at least one quarry. More surprisingly, it can be found in some abundance in southern Ireland. A study made in 1970[4] established that there were no less than 32 churches and five castles in which Dundry stone had been used between 1075 and 1400. Again we see how access to waterborne transport determined the distance a stone could travel. The quarries were close to the Bristol Avon and the sea: the sites where the stone was used are all in the south-east of Ireland in an arc from Drogheda (just north of Dublin) to Kinsale (just south of Cork) and are all close to the sea or to one of the many rivers of this region.

Stone from the Isle of Portland has, perhaps, won more accolades than any other of the region's stones, its reputation spiced by tales of the islanders' insularity of mind and fierceness of independence. Its selection by Wren for the re-built St Paul's turned it into the stone everyone wanted – in London at any rate – though Inigo Jones had actually used it 50 years earlier for the Banqueting House in Whitehall. It is found in three principal beds, the Base bed, the Whit bed and the Roach bed. The Base is regarded as best for carving and the Roach, which Wren used, the strongest. The

Plate 1: Recently quarried Ham Hill Stone (used here as a paving material).

Plate 2: Hamstone ashlar on façade of new house in Long Street, Sherborne.

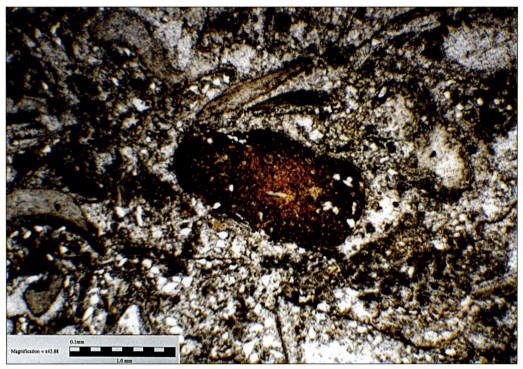

Plate 3: Microscopic sample of Ham Hill Stone showing what seems to be a blob of iron-rich calcareous algae.

Plate 4: An interesting contrast to Ham Hill Stone: Salcombe stone in St Mary & St Peter, Salcombe Regis, Devon.

Plate 5: Hurdwick stone (metamorphosed volcanic ash) with Ham Hill Stone: Town Hall, Tavistock, Devon.

Plate 6: Blue Lias and New Red Sandstone with Hamstone spire: St Mary, Bridgwater.

Plate 7: St Mary, Bridgwater: detail.

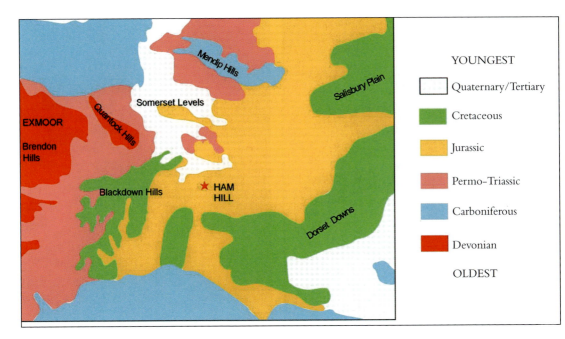

Plate 8: Map 3: Simplified geological map of the region.

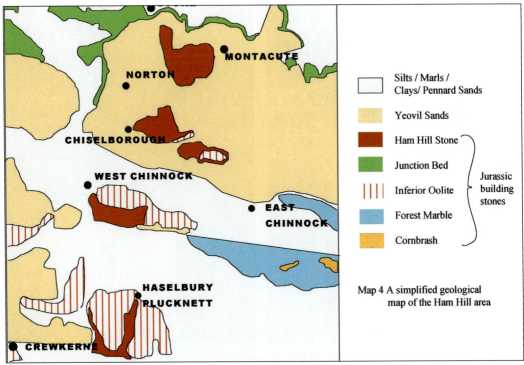

Plate 9: Map 4: Simplified geological map of local area.

Plate 10: Banded flint and Ham Hill Stone: St Peter & St Paul, Cattistock, Dorset.

Plate 11: Chert walls with Hamstone dressings: the Old Grammar School, Chard.

Plate 12: Chalk block with Hamstone dressings: Cattistock, Dorset.

Plate 13: Blue Lias with Hamstone dressings: Somerton.

Plate 14: Ham Hill Stone with banded flint and local stone: St Mary, Stratton, Dorset.

Plate 15: Ham Hill Stone with Portland stone dressings: chimney stacks at Melbury Sampford House, Dorset.

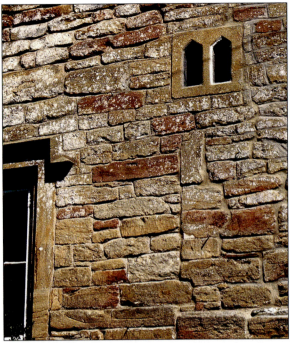

Plate 16: Hamstone cottage in Norton-sub-Hamdon incorporating fire-reddened blocks of stone.

Plate 17: West gateway, Sherborne (Old) Castle with some fine Hamstone masonry.

Plate 18: Hamstone ribs, north aisle, Milton Abbey, Dorset.

Plate 19: Painted Hamstone features, Milton Abbey, Dorset, including figure of St James.

Plate 20: St John, Yeovil (detail): Junction Bed with Hamstone dressings.

Plate 21: St John, Yeovil – Junction Bed with Hamstone dressings: the tower is the earliest of the Perpendicular church towers of Somerset and proved an important influence on later designs.

Plate 22: All Saints, Trull, near Taunton: a typical interior of a Perpendicular-style country church within the 'sphere of influence'.

similar Purbeck-Portland Stone (not to be confused with the Cretaceous Purbeck Stone) had probably been quarried and shipped away to other ports before Portland's reputation was acquired. We have already seen that Salisbury Cathedral's principal building stone is also a form of Portland Stone, the sandier version from the Tisbury/Chilmark area of Wiltshire about 14 miles west of Salisbury. Other versions of Portland Stone used to be quarried at Portesham in Dorset (a few miles west of Portland) where it was used in local buildings, including the sturdy hilltop monument commemorating Admiral Thomas Masterman Hardy (most famous for his captaincy of Nelson's flagship at Trafalgar) who was born and lived in the village below.

There are many less well-known (and less well-travelled) Jurassic limestones in the region which are nevertheless of considerable local importance. In the vicinity of Ham Hill alone, there are several oolitic stones that are all of a gold-ish hue and can easily be confused with Ham Hill Stone at first glance. The first is Sherborne Building Stone, a good quality stone that has been used widely in the town itself and in places around such as Bradford Abbas and Milborne Port. It is a form of what geologists call the Inferior Oolite (Inferior in the sense of being found below the Great Oolite) and a similar form of it was used at Beaminster and the villages around. Next is Forest Marble,[5] the most frequently encountered building stone in west Dorset. In addition to many local quarries, a great deal of it came from Bothenhampton (south of Bridport) where tiles were also made from the upper beds. There is more Inferior Oolite to be found in a north/south formation near Bruton in south Somerset, running parallel to a band of another limestone called Cornbrash (because it yields a brashy soil suitable for growing corn). Cornbrash is also associated with the Great Oolite formations (Bath Stone) in the northern parts of Wiltshire and, in Dorset, with Forest Marble. Yetminster, for example, contains both. Another limestone of local importance is Corallian, which can also be found in north Wiltshire and in two different parts of Dorset – in the north around Sturminster Newton and Stourpaine (where the best is Todber Freestone) and near the coast around Abbotsbury. Abbotsbury itself is an interesting mixture of cream-coloured Corallian, largely re-used from its dissolved monastery, and the greyer Portesham Stone. A similar formation called Coral Rag can be found in north Dorset. Devon simply does not have any of these younger limestones and can lay claim only to limited, and rather poor, deposits of lias near the Dorset border. And it is to lias that we can now turn.

Lower Jurassic or Lias

The most important in this group is, of course, Ham Hill Stone. We have seen how varied it can be in colour and quality. Ham Hill used to be an important source of 'slates' taken from the hard stones of the overburden in the northern spur. Another product of the Hill is the conglomerate that lies between the bottom of the Hamstone bed and the Yeovil Sands below. It is full of pebbles and is very hard.

Coming slightly north of Ham Hill, and stretching intermittently from Corton Denham in the east to Ilchester and Dowlish Wake in the west, is the band of so-called Junction Bed deriving its name from its position between the middle and upper lias beds. It yields the building stone Marlstone, which includes a stone known locally as Moolham Stone. Though it could easily be mistaken for the Inferior Oolite, the way it is configured is entirely different, its surface appearing to consist of a series of swirling circles. It can be seen in Ilminster and also Yeovil, most notably in St John the Baptist church, but also in the outside walls of many of the older buildings. It is noticeable how in all the buildings in which Inferior Oolite, Forest Marble or Junction Bed have been used Ham Hill Stone has still been imported to supply dressings or used more extensively where it could be afforded.

Blue Lias is probably the most common building stone in Somerset. The best of it comes from quarries in the Keinton Mandeville area, but it has been taken out of the ground in many places in the vicinity of Somerton and Street as well as further north towards Bristol. It also appears further south in the Lyme Regis/Seaton area of Dorset and Devon. Though called 'Jurassic' it appears to have little in common with those already considered. It is very distinctly layered consisting of alternating shales and limestones. Its chemical content makes it an excellent source of hydraulic lime. It also makes very good paving stones and is useful for decorative features, but as a building stone it can be porous and rather dull. It is not, indeed, 'the most beguiling of English limestones.'[6] However, it is harsh to generalise as Keinton Mandeville Stone can be used as an attractive 'marble' when polished, and unpolished shafts and other features have been used to good effect in Wells Cathedral and Glastonbury Abbey. In what had once been the magnificent Lady Chapel of the Abbey, there are still some ruined remains of Blue Lias shafts in the blind arcade along the inside walls, contrasting with the creamy Doulting Stone. And we shall see later how it has been used as the perfect foil to Ham Hill Stone in places like Somerton and in some of Somerset's finest Perpendicular Gothic churches. Here the lias is indeed blue-grey but much Blue Lias is not blue at all but yellowy-brown (especially in higher exposed beds). The geologist and author Hugh Prudden has observed that in many new buildings the different colours have been used in a chequerboard style that 'is not to everyone's taste'.[7] The stone commonly referred to as 'White Lias' from the area around Radstock (south of Bath) and from near Langport is not now regarded as true Lias (in the sense of Lower Jurassic) but of older Triassic origin and is more like soft sandstone in consistency. Both Blue and White Lias can be found in Bath in quiet corners away from the fashionable streets all faced in Bath

Stone. It was originally used for flagstones, but later the favoured stone for this was Pennant Sandstone mentioned earlier.

Carboniferous

Oldest of all the limestones is the Carboniferous; in our region it is primarily found in the Mendips. It is what has given these hills their features and character: Cheddar Gorge, the caves at Cheddar and Wookey Hole and the subterranean world that is such a delight to potholers. It is also the rock that is quarried more intensively than any other in the region, not because it is good building stone but because it is in great demand as roadstone. Hence the extensive and controversial quarrying that takes place all over the Mendips, especially in the eastern section of the hills. It is not far from granite in its hardness and is the colour of battleship grey, so it is not an

Map 5: Hamstone country.

Hamstone village name-sign.

Map 5 gives a broad indication of this approach but it must not be taken too literally. In one village there is an interesting change along its main street. In Long Load, north of Martock, the south end of the long north/south street is predominantly of Ham Hill Stone and the north end of Blue Lias. In between, the two stones gradually merge, with sometimes one predominating and sometimes the other. But here we shall confine our attention to places around Ham Hill and its immediate outliers, and then go on to Martock and Crewkerne, followed by a few words on Yeovil. To avoid repetition, it may be taken as read that every building mentioned here is built of Ham Hill Stone in the absence of any indication to the contrary.

But let us not forget the Hill itself. We have seen in Chapter 1 that the only building to have survived from earlier times is the *Prince of Wales* public house and a section of the former 'fair house', which later became a poor house, now incorporated in the garden wall of the pub. The only other buildings (apart from the war memorial which is more closely allied with Stoke than the Hill) are those serving the southern quarry (including an adjoining bungalow containing stone that is mostly artificial!) and a small modern building that serves as the Country Park Ranger's office and public toilets. This is sited near the top of the road that comes up from Stoke but is discreetly tucked away within the mounds of the old workings. A nice touch is that all the functional signs required for the country park ('Lime

Kiln Car Park', 'Norton Car Park', 'No Cycling' and so on) are made from blocks of Ham Hill Stone with incised lettering. The most attractive are those announcing the country park, the one at the foot of the Hill at Little Norton being the most beguiling in its 'fairy dell' setting. The signs were all supplied and carved by the 'harvey' masonry works. A little north of the Deep Quarry are two standing stones called 'The Timestones', sculpted by Eva Bodie to reflect the spirit and historical past of Ham Hill. The circular stone is engraved with intricate patterns that appear on a Celtic artefact (a bucket handle) excavated from the Hill. The other stone is modelled on a Bronze Age axe head, and is so positioned that at sunrise on Midsummer's Day it is lit by the rays of the sun directed through the hole in the circular stone. The stones also represent the start of the 'Liberty Trail', a walking trail to Lyme Regis where the Duke of Monmouth landed in 1685 and gathered local people around him on his ill-fated attempt to take the crown. Whilst there is no suggestion that Ham Hill was a rallying point in the campaign, the stones serve as a reminder that it lay at the heart of a region of England in which the principal events of the rebellion were played out. The final great battle, the last on English soil, took place at Sedgemoor, fifteen miles to the north-west. The most prominent feature in the landscape there is the great Hamstone tower of Westonzoyland Church; the nave of the church was used as a temporary prison to hold the captured survivors of Monmouth's routed army. Another recent feature of the northern spur is a stone circle, rather like a scaled down version of Avebury, consisting of upright and unworked Ham Hill Stone boulders; it has been erected by the quarry company there as an interesting feature for visitors. The northern quarry itself has no associated buildings.

Stoke-sub-Hamdon, lying below the slopes of the northern spur, may lack the elegance of Montacute or the charm of Chiselborough but is full of interest and surprises. It is the village that has been longest and most closely associated with the quarries, and the looming presence of the Hill gives Stoke the air of a mining village in the Pennines or South Wales. The way many of the houses clamber up the Hill adds to the effect. It would be tempting to assume that these were quarrymen's houses, but surprisingly they were built in the 19th century to accommodate workers in the

The 'Timestones' on Ham Hill, sculpted by Eva Bodie: Hamstone carvings inspired by Bronze Age and Celtic artefacts and designed so the rays of the rising sun on Midsummer's Day strike the upright stone through the hole in the circular one.

manor was Arthur, the eldest son of Henry VII. Several buildings in Stoke are still adorned with the Prince of Wales Feathers or with the golden bezants of Cornwall. The Duchy still has a substantial landholding in the parish (about 930 acres) including the northern spur of the Hill.

Another oddity is that it is easy to come away from Stoke without finding its highly regarded Norman church (of which more will be said in the next chapter). The village centre contains a large Congregational church (1865-6) but to find the parish church you must go towards Montacute until you reach East Stoke, a small settlement slightly detached from the main village. The main street along which you pass to reach East Stoke contains several individual houses of some distinction.

Norton-sub-Hamdon, like Stoke, has a long history with some royal connections and a close association with the quarries. And both, of course, are built of Ham Hill Stone. But there any similarities end. The Hill is further away and now presents its long western flank, just one part of a pleasant hilly landscape to the east. And it is laid out in a more traditional way, with the parish church assuming a more central position – and a prominent one too, on a slight rise, and with a magnificent Perpendicular tower making it the grandest of the churches in the Hamstone villages. This may have been influenced by the royal connection with Norton at that time: Henry VII had become Lord of the Manor in the place of Edmund de la Pole (whose dynastic claims Henry feared) and was in a position to act as a benefactor when the old Norman church was rebuilt. He may have been motivated by gratitude for Somerset's support to the Lancastrian cause, as well as following the medieval tradition of paying for good works in one's old age to ease the path to Paradise. Hard by the church stands an ancient dovecote, older than the present church. In a village of many charming nooks and vistas, two great houses stand out – the Manor House at the west end of the village and (nearer to the church) Courtfield, once the home of Charles Trask (see p. 55). Both date from the 17th century.

To the west, and hard against the south-west shoulder of the Hill, lies Little Norton with its former mill (the mill wheel restored to working order) and cluster of houses. In recent years it has attracted unwanted publicity on account of the settlement in the woodland on the southern slope of the Hill (Norton Covert), usually referred to as 'Tinkers' Bubble' after the natural spring that flows all the year at the foot of the slope. The residents of the settlement, who own the land, fought long and hard to be allowed to live an 'alternative' and self-sufficient lifestyle in dwellings that would normally be regarded as 'sub-standard' or even primitive. Planning permission was granted in 1998 on a trial basis for five years. This is not, of course, the first settlement to have been created on the southern slopes of Ham Hill. Only a quarter of a mile away lies the site of Witcombe abandoned 300 years or more ago.

Continuing southwards you come to Chiselborough, the village of the three hills, Gawler's, Balham and Brympton, the last with the shape of a small extinct volcano. The village centre stands on the level ground to the west of the hills and the 13th-century parish church lies on the western edge. The church has a spire (rare in these parts) and a curious one too, bulging in the middle giving it a faintly comical appearance. The land beyond is liable to flood in winter so the rest of the village lies mainly to the east, its cottages (several of them still thatched) delightfully scattered along the valleys and the lower slopes of the hills. 'Still' thatched, because the use of thatch was once more common throughout the Hamstone villages. A regular feature of cottages in the area is the stepped gable edge, usually a sign that the roof was once thatched, the roofing material rising to the full height of the gable edges at each end. Where the thatch has been replaced by slates or tiles, the gable edge stands proud of the roof. Ham Hill Stone has been used generously throughout the village, but its highest

Terraced cottages in West Chinnock (c. 1840): Inferior Oolite with Hamstone dressings and weighty ashlar quoins.

83

is no longer available. A large worked-out quarry can be found at the end of Lyewater leading from the road to Chard. The best of the Hamstone buildings can be found in the areas already mentioned. Brick had come into use here by the middle of the 19th century and was widely used thereafter. It is often used with Hamstone dressings but the mixture is not always a visual success. There is great deal of composite stone but more local stone has started to be used again in recent years. The HSBC bank near the Town Hall has been faced in Guiting Stone, an oolitic limestone from the Cotswolds, but it does not look out of place; the same type of stone was, after all, used in the restoration work of Montacute House (see pp. 205-6). So Crewkerne may not be 'wall-to-wall' Ham Hill Stone like some of the Hamstone villages, but there is still a great deal of it.

Yeovil is the 'capital' of South Somerset and an important manufacturing and trading centre with a population of about 40,000.[10] Architecturally, there is only one building of importance, the church of St John the Baptist, which, like Bath Abbey, has been dubbed 'The Lantern of The West' on account of its great Perpendicular windows (see Chapter 9). However it is a town that you feel would have had more to offer, say, 100 years ago. Yet Edward Hutton's judgment in 1912 was as follows: 'Yeovil, I think, is the most disappointing town in Somerset for apart from its church and a couple of old inns it has practically nothing of antiquity to offer us.'[11]

But, even though both of the 'old inns' have since disappeared,[12] we would, I think, take a much less harsh view of Yeovil today. For a start, Hutton largely ignores anything Georgian or Victorian as being of insufficient 'antiquity' and there are fine Georgian buildings in the street known as Hendford and around the church. Also, since his time notable developments have been carried out in King George Street and in the Quedam Centre. The Town Council have sufficient confidence in Yeovil's historical interest to have produced a Historic Plaque Trail of 25 buildings on which informative blue plaques have been attached.

The local stone is Junction Bed and much is to be found in the older part of the town, invariably with Ham Hill Stone dressings. There are a significant number of buildings with ashlar Hamstone facings but it is a relatively low proportion. The former Baptist church in South Street converted to flats in 2003-4 is notable for having quoins and dressings in Bath Stone with walls of Hamstone ashlar with distinct vertical tooling. Bath Stone was the facing material favoured for the buildings in the prestigious King George Street, but when a new clock tower was built at the end of South Street to mark the Millennium, the chosen material was Ham Hill Stone.

7

Romans, Saxons and Normans

The area around Ham Hill was always likely to be of interest to the Roman invaders. We have seen that it had been of great significance on account of its location since Neolithic times. But this was not all. In a recent study of Roman Somerset Peter Leach draws attention to other advantages:

> South Somerset is a land of broad fertile valleys and rolling limestone hills. For the 2,500 years that divide the Late Bronze Age (1000 BC) from the early post-medieval period (1500 AD) it remained the wealthiest and most densely populated part of the county.[1]

Ham Hill itself was quickly occupied as a defensive site and continued to be occupied even after the town of Ilchester was created 4^1/$_2$ miles away to the north-east. The town, known as Lendiniae (or, perhaps, Lindinis – the only evidence is from scraps of stone from the area of Hadrian's Wall rather than the town itself), lay on the Fosse Way whose existence conferred further advantages for the locality in terms of trade and communications. In the early days of the occupation, Ham Hill and Ilchester would have been regarded as northern outposts of the *civitas* (rather like a county today) that had been established from the area formerly controlled by the Durotriges. The capital of the *civitas* was Dorchester, which was linked to Ilchester by a new road. Moreover, the Fosse Way originally constituted the boundary of the province of Britannia, running from Lincoln to Seaton in Devon. Thus, in the early days a soldier looking north or west from the top of Ham Hill would have been gazing over 'wild' unconquered territory. But once it was all assimilated into a wider province the *Pax Romana* and the prosperity that went with it would prevail.

More than 30 villas in Somerset have been identified as lying within 10 miles of Ilchester, one of the greatest concentrations of villas in England.[2]

Saxon Hamstone quoins, west end St Michael, East Coker, showing a form of long and short work and characteristic Saxon tooling.

Levels (the name means 'big island') and pre-dating the abbey founded by Alfred on the Isle of Athelney to the north. The medieval ruins contain Ham Hill Stone but it is only conjecture that it had been used in Saxon times. The foundations of a small Saxon church have been found within the site of the Norman chancel, but later development swallowed up the original monastery and then most of the buildings (including the entire church) were demolished at the Dissolution. However, a factor that makes it possible it had been used is the close proximity of the site to the river Parrett, often regarded as the major traditional supply route for the stone before the coming of the railways.

It was at Athelney that Alfred had recuperated after his defeat at Chippenham, later emerging to defeat the Danes at Edington. Their leader Guthrum was persuaded to adopt the Christian faith and was baptised at Aller, only four miles or so from Muchelney. The church there contains a simple Saxon font – made of a single block of Ham Hill Stone. It is 'disputed', says the notice in the church, whether this is the font at which Guthrum was baptised, but it would be nice to think it was. Aller was the scene of a moving act of political and religious reconciliation of the highest order. As you pass through the village today, you are only advised that it welcomes careful drivers.

Both at Crewkerne and at Yeovil (as at Muchelney) an original Saxon church was replaced by a Norman one, which itself was replaced by a church in Perpendicular style. Such is the scale of the use of Ham Hill Stone in the present church at Crewkerne that it would be surprising if it had not been used from the beginning. It may have been used at East Coker because there is work on the west wall of this Hamstone church that is now regarded as Saxon. Not only are the cornerstones laid in a form of the 'long

St Mary, Stoke-sub-Hamdon: a rare Norman survival in south Somerset.

All Saints, Sutton Bingham: Norman chancel arch.

and short' style that we associate with Saxon work, but the way the blocks have been dressed in situ, with the tooling marks sweeping from one stone to another, is also typically Saxon. Many of the stones that can be inspected from the ground appear to be of another form of limestone, but some have the shelly characteristic of Ham Hill Stone. Scientific analysis, as was undertaken at Sherborne Abbey (see footnote 16) would settle the issue if an opportunity to take samples arose.

There is more to be seen as we approach the Norman Conquest. St John's church at Milborne Port, east of Sherborne, is, in Professor Pevsner's words, 'historically remarkable for its Saxo–Norman "overlap"'.[17] Typical Saxon pilaster strips can be seen in the exterior south chancel wall alongside Norman features, and parts of the chancel have a Saxon 'feel' although the church is essentially early Norman. Ham Hill Stone has been used for some of the external features but there is none inside; this tells us that it was presumably regarded as harder-wearing than the local (Sherborne) stone but that costs were kept down by not using more than was necessary!

Another church that is Norman but with Saxon overtones is St Mary, Stoke-sub-Hamdon. It is a wonder that the church has survived in its present state. The prosperity of the region in the later Middle Ages fed a church-building mania that led to the disappearance of earlier structures, but Stoke, for some reason, was missed. Perhaps this little church was appreciated even then as being a fine example of its period with its neat proportions, intriguing corbel table and carvings (reminiscent of Kilpeck, Herefordshire) and a breathtaking chancel arch. But the feature for which, perhaps, it is best known is the tympanum over its north door, carved with a child-like simplicity that for many years caused it to be treated as Saxon though it is now believed to be early Norman. It features crude representations of the tree of life, three birds and the Holy Lamb and Cross but also two (but only two) signs of the zodiac – Leo and Sagittarius – each labelled with carvings of their name. The tympanum had been hidden for centuries

Hamstone Norman work at St Andrew, Stogursey, 25 miles from the Ham Hill quarries.

St Andrew, Milborne St Andrew, Dorset: Norman west doorway.

The Conduit, Sherborne in 1910: this was originally the monks' wash-house and stood in the Abbey cloisters.

Plate 23: Sherborne Abbey: crossing pier reddened by the heat of the great fire of 1436; the vertical line on the left shows the position of the pulpitum (since removed).

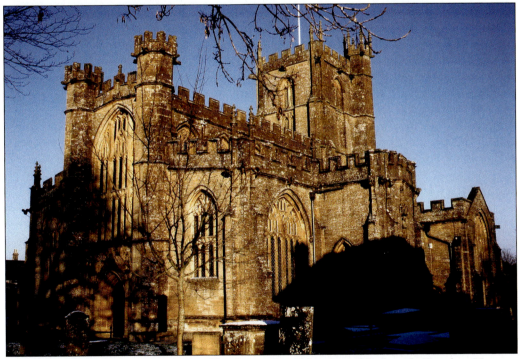

Plate 24: St Bartholomew, Crewkerne: like the medieval churches of Stoke-sub-Hamdon, Norton-sub-Hamdon and Martock, this church was near enough to the quarries to have been built all of Ham Hill Stone.

Plate 28: Melbury House, Melbury Sampford: late 17th-century Classical re-modelling of the Tudor house: Hamstone walls with Portland stone quoins and dressings.

Plate 29: Parnham House, Beaminster, Dorset: early 19th–century extension by John Nash.

Plate 30: Duck House, South Street, Sherborne: an austere Regency design in a bright shade of Ham Hill Stone.

Plate 31: St George, Tiverton, Devon (1714) – a rare example of a Georgian church in the region: the unexpected choice of Ham Hill Stone so far from the quarries may have been influenced by the presence in the town of Old Blundells (1604).

Plate 32: A modest but effective use of polychromy with Blue Lias and Ham Hill Stone: All Saints, Isle Brewers (1861, C. E. Giles).

Plate 33: G. E. Street's St John the Evangelist, Torquay, Devon (with prominent Hamstone dressings) rising above the harbour.

Plate 34: A variety of local granites at Launceston, Cornwall: there seems no need to have imported Ham Hill Stone for use in other buildings here.

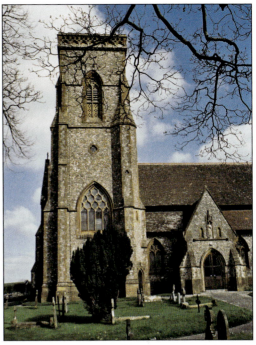

Plate 35: *Hairy Dog* public house, The Avenue, Minehead: Permo-Triassic sandstones with Ham Hill Stone.

Plate 36: St Mary, Buckland St Mary (1853-63, Benjamin Ferrey): Chert with Hamstone dressings.

Plate 37: Palace Court, Moscow Road, Bayswater, London: the shady forecourt of a seven-storey block of flats built in 1880 of brick and ashlar facing blocks mainly of Ham Hill Stone.

Plate 38: The severely weathered Hamstone façade of the George Hotel, Crewkerne contrasting with the adjoining Hamstone façade.

Plate 39: Furrowed stone: part of Ilminster's Georgian Market House.

governing body) of the cathedral. Thus it is that the King's House in the Cathedral Close (the present home of Salisbury and South Wiltshire Museum) was originally called 'Sherborne Place', the Salisbury residence of the Abbot. It began as quite a small building (and no doubt there had been an equivalent building at Old Sarum) but it was rebuilt in the form of a hall in the 15th century and it is this north/south range that we see today, despite all the changes and additions that have been made since. The outside front walls contain, amongst a fascinating mixture of different materials, some vestigial remains of Hamstone window dressings, and the entrance porch has a fine display of Ham Hill Stone, including some richly carved ribbed vaulting. We must assume that the Abbot of the day wished to spare no expense in bringing to Salisbury some of the stone which he knew so well in Sherborne (in much the same way as the first Norman settlers in England made extensive use of stone from Caen in Normandy), because to transport the stone from Ham Hill would have been very costly indeed. We saw (p. 48) that the Ham Hill Stone used for the Almshouse of SS. John in Sherborne (also in the 15th century) cost 12d per load to purchase and 1s.8d per load to haul overland from the quarries about ten miles away. Salisbury is at least four times this distance from Ham Hill and the costs would probably increase disproportionately with at least three or four overnight stops. A study of the distribution pattern of Ham Hill Stone suggests that the normal distance for the transport of goods in one day in medieval times was '12km' (7½ miles).[9] However, because of the way that the stone at the King's House was used with other, more local, materials, it is possible that only a few loads of it would have been required. Both Salisbury and Yeovil stand on one of the traditional routes between London and Penzance (corresponding to the present-day A30) and this is likely to be the route by which the Abbot's precious stone was transported.

The way places of prestige are able to attract fine building materials from far away seems to operate rather like the laws of gravity: the greater the wealth and importance, the greater the pulling power. And next to cathedrals in importance came the monasteries. The hugely wealthy abbeys of Glastonbury (which, in any case, owned its own quarries at Doulting) and Shaftesbury were a little too far away to be relevant to our story, but there are several nearer ones that are, namely, Milton, Cerne, Forde, Muchelney and Sherborne (though not Abbotsbury, which relied entirely on more local stone).

The abbey church at Milton, 'a miniature cathedral in a vast green bowl',[10] survived both the Dissolution and the depredations to the little town of Milton by Joseph Damer (later Lord Dorchester) in the 18th century. The abbey had been founded in 933; its church was destroyed in a storm in 1309 and rebuilt in the 14th and 15th centuries. Curiously, the church consists of a crossing and a huge aisled chancel but no nave. There had been no time to complete it before Henry VIII put an end to the

Sandford Orcas Manor, Dorset (16th century): an archetypal Tudor manor house built in an unusual grey shade of Ham Hill Stone, as photographed in 1939 when ivy-clad walls were more fashionable than they are today for older buildings.

It has already been noted that at the manor house of Bingham's Melcombe Renaissance motifs had been adopted in a part of the house that had been 'certainly completed by 1561'.[2] As a demonstration of how advanced this was we only need to compare it with East Lambrook Manor of 1584, which at its east end contains an upper floor Gothic window, its two lights cusped and pointed.

There then follows what John Newman describes as a 'group of architecturally inventive houses in Somerset and Dorset designed by a master-mason or masons based at Hamdon Hill'.[3] At first he appears to have only three in mind, Barrington Court, Melbury Sampford and Clifton Maybank, but it becomes clear later that he would also include Mapperton House and Athelhampton House (and Hinton House may be another). The revealing features that tie these houses together stylistically are 'octagonal angle shafts, their faces hollowed, and the barley sugar finials'.[4] Barrington Court was acquired by the National Trust in 1907 but only restored in the

Barrington Court (c. 1550?) with its mottled Hamstone walls and rare blend of Gothic and Renaissance styles.

1920s by Col. A. A. Lyle. It was probably built in its present form from about 1550, though there is a possibility that it was earlier. There has also been much dissension about its style, whether it represents one of the last examples of medieval Gothic or one of the first Renaissance buildings. It is easier to regard it as one of many good examples of the peculiarly *English* style – a unique blend of traditional native idioms infused with fledgling, and often misunderstood, Renaissance motifs – that prevailed in the second half of the 16th century and gave us masterpieces as diverse as Hardwick Hall, Derbyshire, Wollaton Hall, Nottingham and, at the very end of that period, Montacute House.

Athelhampton House, near Dorchester, is another property that is open to the public for most months of the year. The original range, containing the Great Hall, was built in about 1485 by Sir William Martyn, a successful merchant who became Lord Mayor of London in 1492. It was built entirely of grey Portesham Stone. But in the second quarter of the 16th century[5] a south range was added that incorporated Ham Hill Stone for its impressive range of mullioned windows (the largest also has transoms). It contains octagonal corner buttresses and twisted finials (all with concave faces) that are the tell-tale sign that this range belongs to a group of 16th-century buildings 'for which design as well as stone seems to have come from Hamdon Hill, Somerset'.[6] It is also a remarkable example of how the warmth of the stone has affected the character not just of the 16th-century range but of the entire ensemble. A great deal more Ham Hill Stone has been used in later portions of the house as well as throughout its well-known gardens. The property is managed with pride and sensitivity by the Cooke family who first acquired it in 1957.

A house that may be enjoyed from the outside when its gardens are open is Mapperton House, just east of Beaminster. It has its full measure of

Mapperton House, Dorset (16th century): its twisted Hamstone finials are a feature of a group of houses in the region built at this time by masons from Ham Hill.

'barley sugar finials' but it is all on a smaller scale than Barrington and the sense of enclosure given by the L shape of the house, the little adjoining church and the service buildings on the opposite side of the driveway – themselves of much architectural interest – gives it a more intimate feel. There is a most confusing mix here of Ham Hill Stone and the local Inferior Oolite but the broad pattern of use appears to be that the original house was Hamstone (supporting the 'Ham Hill masons' theory) and that all later work was either in local stone alone or with Hamstone dressings. Its roof is covered with stone slates from Ham Hill but 'it is not known whether they are an original feature or later repairs.'[7]

Melbury Sampford is probably the earliest of them all, being newly built when John Leland saw it in 1540. The house has undergone considerable alteration, but the large size and grandeur of the original building is still evident from the surviving gabled walls and its unusual and noble hexagonal prospect tower that passes up through one side of the original house. Most of the tower's decorative detail has been replaced (probably for

Barrington Court: a detail showing the twisted and hollow-faced elements used by the Ham Hill masons.

the most part in the 19th century) but there is one chimney (close to the tower) with a zigzag design that is probably original. The twisted finial became the *leitmotif* for the house, appearing in abundance on balustrades and rooflines in all its subsequent phases. Architecturally, the richest of all had been Clifton Maybank, but most of it was demolished in the 18th century and what remains is a shapeless lump compared with what it must once have been. But thanks to Edward Phelips V of Montacute House (he who built the observatory tower on St Michael's Hill), we may still see some of the best work because he purchased part of the stone fabric of Clifton Maybank while it was being demolished and incorporated it into a new west front that he gave Montacute between 1785 and 1788. A sixth house that might well have received the attentions of the Ham Hill team is Hinton House. The contemporary depictions of the Tudor house do not show any twisted finials but the private 'museum' within the house has a section of carving (about half a metre long) of the same concave spiral design as used in the other five houses.

Did the craftsmen responsible for this group of houses arrive at Ham Hill at the right moment to build in this new style? It is far more likely that they were either the same men who, right up to the early rumblings of the Dissolution, were working from time to time on prestigious monastery buildings or churches, or younger men who learnt their skills. That these men 'had a way with stone' is clearly evident from what we still see in Late Gothic work at, for example, Forde Abbey, Montacute Priory and the churches of Norton-sub-Hamdon and Crewkerne. It is unlikely that they would initiate stylistic innovations themselves but would be content to follow whatever template or more general guidance they were given by their patron or master mason. Thus it would not take long to master the three-dimensional movement of the spiral motifs used in these four houses or to direct their carving skills to other rudimentary Renaissance

Prospect Tower, Melbury House, Melbury Sampford, Dorset: the principal surviving feature of the Tudor house, which was probably the earliest of the 'Ham Hill' group.

Montacute House, Somerset (commenced c. 1580): part of the additions to the west front from the earlier Clifton Maybank.

135

motifs. And we have already noted that the skills required to produce fine ashlar masonry, a feature of all five houses, had existed since late Norman times. Yet this does not account for the rich display of Renaissance features in the relief panel on the west front at Montacute House that was originally carved for Clifton Maybank. The quality of the carving is so exceptional that it has been attributed to French masons; and it has been argued that the inferior quality of figure carving on the (later) east front of Montacute House is 'surely the work of local masons'.[8] The panel was probably made not later than 1550 and the frieze of the panel consists of Gothic tracery and shields, demonstrating that the carvers (whether French or English) were at that time switching from one style to the other. Yet another mansion of the mid-16th century is Parnham House near Beaminster, though it may have been built entirely of Inferior Oolite and, in any event, the original parts have been rather swamped by later alterations and additions. Much the same is true of Dillington House (now Somerset County Council's Adult Training Centre) near Whitelackington. It may have begun life in about 1550 but in the 1830s was restored and altered on a large scale, though preserving the general appearance of an Elizabethan (or, perhaps, Jacobean) mansion.

Examples of genuine Hamstone Elizabethan houses can be found in the main street of Chard (Fore Street), namely, the former Grammar School at the lower (eastern) end and Court House further up on the same (northern) side. The first of these, which did not come to be used as a school until 1671, was built in 1583. The Court House is a little later and rather more complex, consisting of what had been two houses around a courtyard. They are delightful examples, first, of houses in a vernacular style that originated from the early 15th century, that would barely change over the following 250 years or so and would continue to be influential into the 19th century and (through the Arts and Crafts movement) even beyond:

The Old Grammar School, Chard, Somerset (1583) - Chert with Hamstone dressings: built originally as a house in a vernacular style (with gables and mullioned windows) that prevailed for about 250 years.

Wigborough Manor House, Somerset (1585): its vernacular style gives the building a solid and timeless quality and its Hamstone ashlar a touch of distinction.

that is to say, with gables and mullioned windows –
usually with 'labels' over them – and all of a simple,
unpretentious yet dignified design. The Priory
(probably a former manor house) in Hinton St
George, rebuilt in the middle of the 17th century, and
the Manor House of 1679 in Martock's main street
are two cases in point and we shall see the same style
being revived, or perhaps it is better to say 'continued',
by A. W. N. Pugin in the 19th century. But, secondly,
they are even finer examples of buildings faced with
knapped chert with Hamstone dressings – a pleasing
combination that is a common feature of buildings in
and around Chard. Two rural examples of Elizabethan
houses in south Somerset are North Cadbury Court
(of perhaps 1581) and Wigborough Manor House
(1585). Cadbury has, one suspects, always been the
'classier' of the two, having been modernised with a
Classical south-facing frontage in the 18th century.
Wigborough forms part of a working farm and has
more of a timeless vernacular quality.

*Montacute House: east front (commenced
c.1580): a dignified essay in Ham Hill
Stone on a magnificent scale.*

And so to Montacute House, perhaps the best-
known Hamstone building of all because it has all the style and panache
one would expect in an Elizabethan 'prodigy' house yet shares the
timelessness of Wigborough, having an almost vernacular feel of its own. In
terms of style, Montacute is almost as remote from being a true 'Classical'
building, based on the precepts of Roman architecture, as the group of five
mid-16th-century buildings considered earlier. The most convincing
Classical features are on the east side – the shell-headed niches in the
ground floor, the round niches in the floor above and the free-standing
columns on the steps. Yet the general structure is based on a large amount
of window space in the Gothic manner (if not quite to the extent of
Hardwick Hall) and other decorative features are either Flemish in origin
or show only a passing similarity to anything Roman – notably the statues
of the Nine Worthies along the uppermost floor of the east front. Their
vaguely Roman dress announces a wish on the part of the owner to appear
fashionable but they look more like clumsy dolls than Roman statues. Yet
the overall effect is one of dignified magnificence.

The Phelips family for whom it was built had been associated with the
Montacute area since the 15th century but work did not begin on the
house until perhaps 1590 or so, finishing probably in 1601. The builder was
the first Edward Phelips who had a distinguished legal career and became
Speaker of the House of Commons in 1604. The man whom Phelips
employed as architect (so far as one may use that term in an age before it
was used in its modern sense) was 'almost certainly'[9] the Somerset mason

William Arnold, recommended to him by Dorothy Wadham who later used Arnold for Wadham College, Oxford. The result, at any rate, is one of England's most important houses architecturally; and its rich simplicity gives it a closer affinity to the modern age than to any of the periods of revivalism that would follow. There is the sense that, with the right modern materials, the builders could have stepped from 1600 to 2000 without effort, or the need to know what had happened in between.

An essential part of the 'Montacute experience' is the way that (with two interesting exceptions mentioned later) every element and decorative feature of the principal building (including the wide steps and columns on the east side) and every lodge and pavilion and garden wall down to the last finial and baluster is made of Ham Hill Stone. Even the two staircases – the northern one being on an especially spacious scale – are of stone rather than of timber, which was starting to become fashionable elsewhere.[10] As Lady Macbeth nearly said: who would have thought the old Hill to have had so much stone in it? The exceptions occur in the two most prominent rooms of the house. The Great Hall contains an elaborate Renaissance-style stone screen, which is Hamstone except for its frieze and for the capitals of its attached columns. These are made of Portland Stone, and the contrast in colour is most effective. And Portland Stone is used again in the Library (formerly the Great Chamber) for the monumental chimneypiece that is its dominant feature. Phelips appears to be saying to his visitors that although he has used local stone to build his house he can also afford to use stone that is a great deal more expensive on account of the distance it has had to be transported overland.

One special feature of the house is the Long Gallery, the longest in England, which takes up the entire length of the second floor. It is expressed in the outward design by the graceful oriels at that level at the north and south ends. As one might guess from the way that the typical Elizabethan E shape of the house faces east, as well as from the way the great set of shallow steps leads up to the entrance on that side, access to the house was originally from the east. It was Edward Phelips V who, as well as making additions to the west front (including the incorporation of stone fabric from Clifton Maybank), created the western drive (no longer used) so that the approach could be from the west. The main point behind this is that it distanced the house from the public highway, which hitherto had run close to the house on the eastern side.[11] The pavilions at the far corners of the walled east garden – and indeed the walling itself with its balustrade and lanterns and obelisks – are significant Hamstone structures in their own right. Equally splendid is the lodge towards the centre of the village.

All this splendour would have been even more impressive in its day when it was something new. Thomas Coryate, the great 17th-century traveller from nearby Odcombe, had been the godson of Thomas Phelips (Edward's father) and had probably seen the house being built. He was certainly impressed by it, for while in Germany he would not stand for the suggestion that a particular building there was finer than anything in England:

> ... there is one in mine own country of Somersetshire, even the magnificent house of my most worthy and right Worshipful neighbour and Mecoenas, Sir Edward Phillippes, now maister of the Rolles (whome I name honoris causâ) in the town of Montacute, so stately adorned with the statues of the nine Worthies, that may be at the least equally ranked with [this German building] if not something preferred before it.[12]

Wayford Manor (south-west of Crewkerne) was built at about the same time as Montacute and, shortly afterwards, Newton Surmaville (on the south-eastern fringe of Yeovil yet inaccessible and in a world of its own). William Arnold had gone on to work for the Luttrell family at Dunster Castle in or around 1617. Most of Arnold's exterior work has disappeared under that of Anthony Salvin in the 1870s, but Salvin's work incorporates some Ham Hill Stone and it is not too outlandish to suggest that Arnold had supplies of it as well; the Luttrell Arms Hotel in the village has some of the stone in the upper windows of the entrance porch which is of much the same age as Arnold's work.

Also of 1617 is the Court of Sovereigns, Cadhay, Ottery St Mary, Devon. This was built for Robert Hayden who had married a member of the Poulett family (or Paulett, as they prefer to spell it in Devon), of Hinton

Court of Sovereigns, Cadhay, Ottery St Mary, Devon: it was probably marriage to a Poulett of Hinton St George that led to the use of Ham Hill Stone here in 1617 (see detail in colour section).

Chantmarle House, Dorset (from 1612?) in the regional tradition of Tudor and Jacobean Hamstone manor houses.

House mentioned above, explaining, no doubt, the use of the stone in its fabric. Hayden was building a new wing that would comprise the fourth side of a square, and thus create the court. In the court itself the stone is used for the doorways and as one of the elements in a most unusual chequerboard pattern on all four walls. It can also be detected in the outer wall of the new wing and, more surprisingly, in the outer façade of the opposite wing, which was altered in the 18th century. An important house of this period in Dorset, built probably between 1612 and 1623, is Chantmarle (north of Dorchester), all of Hamstone ashlar and decorative details. It has lost the ends of its original E shape and was given a large extension in 1919 but the building has a gracious air enhanced by the use of a single stone throughout. For many years it was the Dorset Police Training College but has recently (2003) been acquired for use as a Christian Resource Centre. Sir Walter Raleigh began his new mansion, the 'new' Sherborne Castle in about 1594 and, after his downfall in 1617, the work was continued by Lord Digby to whom the Queen had given the lease of the estate. It is an H-shaped building with many interesting features and interiors but oddly unsatisfying, somehow, from the outside. It was unusual for its time in that the stone rubble walls were covered in lime plaster. However, all the dressings as well as the balustrades, heraldic carvings and elaborate stone gateways are of exposed natural stone, which, of course, came from Ham Hill.

The loss of the monasteries entailed the loss of monastic schools and the need for them to be replaced by other establishments. One of the best known of the schools established under the patronage of Edward VI was Sherborne, whose Arms remain those of that monarch. We have seen how the Abbey church was acquired by the townsfolk, and in a town that was still very small this great building would have been a community facility used for a variety of purposes apart from regular church services and private worship. It was therefore perfectly natural that a new school for the town should be located in the church. And it is clear, even from the outside, just where it was located. As you proceed eastwards along the south side of the church, the Perpendicular gives way to a section in Renaissance style incorporating a splendid carving of the Royal Arms of Edward VI. On the other side of this wall within the church lay the Headmaster's residence, conveniently placed for the education of pupils within the precinct of the

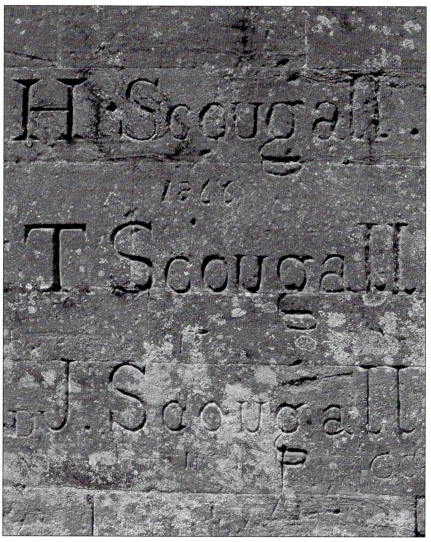

Schoolboys' graffiti on main façade of Old Blundells, Tiverton, Devon (1604) consisting entirely of Ham Hill Stone.

church. All this occurred in 1560 but it would not be long before a purpose-built school would be provided within the site of the former monastery at the east end of the church. This is what is now known as the School House Dining Hall built in 1606-8. Though only a few years after Montacute was completed, the Classical nature of the building is much more evident with the sophistication of an Ionic order superimposed on a Doric order.

Yet Blundells School at Tiverton, Devon completed in 1604, is 'entirely unclassical'[13] apart from the round-arched doorways. Perhaps this comes as no surprise in a location even further removed from court circles than Sherborne, but the fact that it is built of Ham Hill Stone, at this early date,

The Mansion, Evershot, Dorset - Forest Marble with Hamstone dressings: a showy 'urban' façade in a village setting.

is now a hotel and featured as the manor house in BBC TV's comedy series *To the Manor Born*. A stone column high in the hills above Compton Dundon commemorates the more famous Admiral Samuel Hood, brother of Alexander. Pitt's house at Cricket Malherbie was built in about 1820 and, it is said, to his own plan. 'The appearance of the house,' says Professor Pevsner, 'makes that probable.'[6] Externally it uses Greek Doric features – heavy columns, tapering doorframes, curious pieces of frieze over the window and weird extended triglyphs within the central pediment. Inside, reports Pevsner, an Ionic capital split by a door is 'a painful sight'. St Thomas uses Hamstone ashlar throughout; Malherbie has rendered walls but with Hamstone columns and dressings. An early Georgian house of greater sophistication than one would expect to find in a village is The Mansion, Evershot. All its dressings and Classical features are Hamstone including the distinctive grotesque mask carved on the keystone over the doorway. Parnham House was considerably altered and extended between 1807 and 1811. The architect was John Nash, who sought to maintain the Tudor style with gables rising above a battlemented parapet, large windows (with mullions and transoms) and buttresses topped with tall finials wearing 'coolie hats' (BoE). Some Ham Hill Stone was used alongside the local Inferior Oolite.

The 18th century, more than any other, was the age of the folly. Wealthy landowners of the time built their Palladian country houses to demonstrate respectability and refinement but showed their desire for pleasure and

The Mansion, Evershot: detail.

frivolity by building follies. Nothing could be more frivolous than the four follies of Barwick Park set at the four points of the compass from Barwick House (near Yeovil) and known as The Obelisk, the Fish Tower, the Rose Tower (or Messiter's Cone) and Jack the Treacle Eater. Neither Hutton (1912) nor Mee (in *The King's England*, 1939) mention them, a sign perhaps that follies fell out of favour in later times and were not seriously

148

The Barwick Follies, near Yeovil: built of locally-quarried stone with dressed features in Ham Hill Stone.

regarded. Pevsner has a brief reference to three of them ('*c*.1830'). But Headley and Meulenkamp writing in 1999 deal with them at some length ('Somerset's finest folly achievement').[7] They refer to a painting of *c*.1770, in which two of them appear, as evidence that they were built earlier than had generally been thought. The Barwick follies are made mostly of a poor local stone quarried on the estate but Hamstone has been used for the finer dressed features, including, for example, the uppermost Gothick-style tier of the Fish Tower.

Edward Phelips's tower on the top of St Michael's Hill at Montacute is usually described as a folly but it may have been a more serious venture – certainly a place from which to view the surrounding countryside ('periskopein' appears in a Greek inscription over the doorway) and very likely too a place from which to study the heavens at night, an observatory. It is faced with finely jointed Hamstone ashlar. A 'folly' in a more general sense concerns a house called 'Follys' (now 'Homefield'), Rectory Lane, Norton-sub-Hamdon. Headley and Meulenkamp incorrectly describe it as 'Little Follys' and as being in Martock but the substance of the tale they tell is true enough: that it was built by the quarry proprietor, Richard England (with 'a good name for the quality of his stonework'), partly from stone from a derelict cottage (unlisted) on another site in the village. Soon afterwards, in 1961, it was listed (and remains listed) as 'a detached house, formerly subdivided. C17 and later, but possibly with earlier fragments.'[8]

Looking now at towns, Yeovil (as noted in Chapter 6) has a good legacy of Georgian buildings. Most are of the local stone from the Junction Bed with Hamstone dressings but a number have an entire Hamstone frontage with ashlar walls. One is Hendford Manor House (1760) – impressive from a distance, though on closer inspection it becomes apparent that much of

Falkland House, Crewkerne: fine Hamstone ashlar.

the ashlar was laid face-bedded and that large swathes of the surface of the stone have had to be repaired with lime mortar. The Baroque porch is presumably late 19th century or after. Its current use is as offices and its former coach house also has a new lease of life housing Yeovil Museum, in an isolated situation in the middle of a large public car park. The building was never designed for such exposure but its strong Classical design in a good red brick with heavy Hamstone quoins and window surrounds is enough to carry it off. The Manor Hotel on the other side of Hendford was built in 1776 as a home for a gentleman described in its 'blue plaque' as a local glover and merchant banker. An interesting feature is that the finely carved Ionic capitals of the columns of the attached portico are of Portland Stone whereas the rest of the façade is entirely of Ham Hill Stone. In view of the superiority of Portland for intricate carving (as well as the Montacute precedent (see p. 138)), it is surprising, perhaps, that this approach did not catch on. The results might have been interesting. Princes Street and Church Street both contain Georgian buildings, by far the most notable being Church House, built in 1750 (in red brick with Hamstone dressings) as a home for a 'family of solicitors' (according to its blue plaque) and now in use as offices. One building from the 17th century is the *Three Choughs* Inn, with Hamstone bolection mouldings and (badly pointed) walls of Junction Bed Stone.

Ilminster is a small town by today's standards but its buildings indicate a past prosperity offering an interesting contrast with its near namesake, Ilchester, which never recaptured the importance it enjoyed in Roman times. Indeed, when Leland passed through Ilchester in 1542, he reported that it 'used to be a very large affair, and one of the oldest towns in the whole region. But now it has fallen into spectacular decay, almost as if it had been devastated by an army'.[9] Ilchester may have two medieval churches[10] but they are far outstripped in magnificence by St Mary, Ilminster. And it is in the buildings of the Georgian era that the contrast is again evident. Ilminster's principal streets seem packed with buildings of this age whose builders were able to afford a full Hamstone façade. The best are in Silver Street – Ashleigh House, Somerset House and the large solicitors' offices (18-20) next to the churchyard. Its open-sided Market House is also made entirely of the stone. By contrast, Ilchester has only 'The

Elms', High Street, where its Hamstone ashlar frontage stands out among the mainly Blue Lias buildings around it. Ilminster's local stone was by no means eschewed completely (the George Hotel is built of it)[11] but it does not predominate in the way that Blue Lias does in Ilchester – even though Ilchester lies 3-4 miles nearer to Ham Hill. However, Hamstone dressings are used a great deal in Ilchester, a combination that usually works well. The modest *Dolphin* public house in High Street, for example, has much greater charm than the Ilchester Arms Hotel whose Hamstone Doric portico is a grand feature in itself but does not blend happily with the red brick walls. During the Regency period, Liongate House on the east side of the town (just beyond the River Yeo) was given a sophisticated façade in fashionable Greek, including a porch with two Doric columns *in antis* (i.e. within the entrance). But it is all in Bath Stone, an indication perhaps that the designer did not feel that Ham Hill Stone would be suitable for the refined coolness that he was trying to achieve. And the fact that it is a façade is clear from the western wall, which is in a much earlier vernacular style, with Hamstone window dressings in a wall of Blue Lias. The lias/Hamstone combination was also used successfully in a number of Somerton's Georgian buildings, not least its parish church and its distinctive Market Cross.

Crewkerne has a high proportion of Georgian buildings, paid for by its renewed prosperity from the sailcloth trade. The best, and all with elegant ashlar walls, are in Church Street, in High Street (Falkland House) and in East Street. Merefield House, East Street has a 'Soanean' air about it and it is not unreasonable to speculate whether Soane had a hand in it while working at nearby Cricket St Thomas. One of the most striking buildings in the town is the George Hotel in the Market Square, not so much for its Georgian architecture as for the worn and fractured appearance of its masonry – a severe example of the damage that can be caused by atmospheric pollution and contrasting oddly with the still smooth ashlar of the neighbouring Lloyds TSB bank.

Martock has a number of good buildings from the Age of Elegance: its Town Hall distinctively raised on open arches and with a Venetian window overlooking the 18th-century fluted column, on a medieval base, known as 'The Pinnacle' (recently knocked down by a lorry for the third time in living memory), as well as several houses (some in Bower Hinton) with the Classical porches that were so fashionable at that time. Two interesting buildings from the Regency period when (architectural) 'chastity' was in vogue are Ashfields (now surrounded by houses built in its former grounds) with simple lines and widely spaced Greek Doric columns *in antis*; and, even more austere, Moorlands House (near the Library) with smooth ashlar walls and a semi-circular-headed doorway (in finely shaped and fitted Ham Hill Stone) with a pair of Greek Doric columns within the space supporting a thin slab of stone with nothing above it; very curious. And of

Moorlands House, Martock; the modern fittings do not aspire to match the high quality of the Hamstone masonry in this curious Regency Greek design.

1840 (though mentioned here on account of its late Classical style) is Bridge House with its impressive bowed array of Venetian windows. This was the home of William Wynne Westcott, a leading freemason and mystic of his time.[12]

It will come as no surprise that Sherborne has some fine examples of this era: Sherborne House, Newlands (the former Lord Digby's School now awaiting transformation into an arts centre for the town) designed by Benjamin Bastard and built in about 1720; Red House, Long Street, red brick and Sherborne Building Stone with Ham Hill Stone used only in garden features and in the quoins of a later extension at the rear; Duck House, South Street in a chaste Regency style with round-topped windows set in brightly coloured Hamstone ashlar; and a little lower down the street a house (now a nursing home) with a richly carved porch incorporating rusticated columns. Many of its more modest houses in the central streets are also from this period, mostly of the local stone with Hamstone quoins and dressings.

Churches of this period require separate attention because of their variety. Classical-style churches are rare. The most significant is St George, Tiverton in Devon. It was begun in about 1714 on a prominent central site in the town to the design of John James – an architect much influenced by Inigo Jones – and who produced plain and sturdy Palladian designs. His choice of material for the entire exterior, ashlared walls, quoins, dressings and carved details (such as they are) is Ham Hill Stone, being influenced, possibly, by Blundells School at the other end of the main street. The total

Left: Bridge House, Martock (1840), home of a leading 19th-century Freemason and mystic.
Right: Sherborne House, Sherborne (1720, Benjamin Bastard): Hamstone dressings used for this former stately residence, later a school and now an arts centre.

effect is one of great elegance. It is 'Devon's best C18 town church'.[13] The Meeting Room at Ilminster (all of Ham Hill Stone) was built in 1718-19; its general appearance is that of an early Georgian building yet Gothic lingers in the slightly arched tops of the windows. A good example of a Nonconformist chapel of this period (1729) in a typically simple Classical style can be seen at Mid Lambrook, Somerset. The prevailing Classical style of the age is to be seen more readily (and more widely) in the headstones, tomb chests and memorials in the churches and churchyards throughout the 'sphere of influence'. In 'Hamstone country', where the church itself is of Ham Hill Stone, the effect of an array of golden lichen-covered tomb chests and headstones can be delightful.

Congregational chapel, Mid Lambrook (1729) in a simplified Classical style.

All the other churches worth noting are Gothic; the Gothic tradition would continue well into the 17th century and the style would start to appear again from the middle of the 18th, though by now it would be 'Gothick', a Gothicising of Classical forms. Architectural historian Tim Mowl, in a study entitled

Former Congregational chapel, Long Street, Sherborne (1803): a good example of Georgian Gothick, with Hamstone dressings and details.

St Andrew, Minterne Magna, Dorset: one of a group of Gothic Survival churches in the region, built between 1610 and 1628 and all of local stone with Hamstone dressings.

relatively small amount for his residence in the Cathedral Close. The railway allowed much greater quantities to be brought from the quarries and so when the Wilts and Dorset Bank built its headquarters in Blue Boar Row (now Lloyds TSB), its *palazzo*-style façade was built entirely of Ham Hill Stone. The architect was Henry Hall (1826-1909) whose offices were in London but who did a good deal of work in Somerset and west Dorset including a school at Sherborne (opened in 1857) and, at Milborne Port, a school (1864) and church restoration (1867-69). He would later restore the church at Sandford Orcas (1871). Thus he would have been familiar with the unique qualities of the stone and may have recommended it to the bank (though another possible explanation is explored under 'Bank Buildings' below). Soon afterwards (1874) Ham Hill Stone was used on a lavish scale for a prominent new building at the junction of High Street and Bridge Street to house Richardson's Wine Vaults (now Barclays Bank). The similarities with the Blue Boar Row building point to the architect again being Henry Hall: it is in the style of an Italian *palazzo* (Venetian this time), the head carved into the keystone above the main entrance could be mistaken for the identical feature at the bank, and, of course, it is again in Ham Hill Stone.

This was followed by extensions to the 13th-century almshouse known

Town Hall, Marlborough, Wiltshire (1902, C. E. Ponting): an elaborate display of Ham Hill Stone.

as St Nicholas Hospital (Crickmay & Son, Dorchester, 1885), where it was mixed with flint; the re-building of Taylor's Almshouses (1886), a red brick building with Hamstone quoins and dressings; the new King's Head Inn, Bridge Street (E. Doran Webb, 1893), an Arts and Crafts building entirely faced in Ham Hill Stone;[2] an unusually elegant electricity generating station (1898) adjoining the ancient Town Mill in the centre of town, where it was used for the window surrounds in a façade of brick and flint (as well as in a small related building in St Thomas Square); and finally extensions to the Wilts and Dorset Bank HQ made in two stages – late in the 19th century and in 1901, when at the same time an 'Edwardian Baroque' building (now Lloyds Bank Chambers) was built on the Chipper Lane frontage of the bank's long L-shaped site.

It is interesting that there should be

so many Hamstone buildings in Salisbury when there are none that have been identified in the nearby Hampshire towns of Andover or Winchester, only one in Portsmouth (in part of the Bishop's House next to the Roman Catholic Cathedral) and only two in Southampton.[3] (Even Shaftesbury in Dorset, a great deal nearer to the Hamstone quarries than Salisbury, seems to have relied on a local source of a rather gloomy grey sandstone for its stone-faced buildings with the sole exception of the Georgian Mitre Inn, High Street built of Sherborne Building Stone with Hamstone dressings.)

Nor are there any significant quantities elsewhere in Wiltshire, though the architect C. E. Ponting used it twice – at Pensham House, near Calne (1892) and, in 1902, for the Town Hall, Marlborough, the building that stands prominently at the east end of the town's great High Street. The style is eclectic – mainly Dutch Classical – but with a richly dominant west-facing end feature in a sturdy Renaissance style, consisting of a carved doorway rising into a balcony and bay window (with mullions and transoms) surmounted by a balustrade and armorial feature. Ham Hill Stone was selected for this elaborate display of stonework and was also used for quoins and dressings throughout the building as a whole.

DEVON
Exeter

No doubt it was through the connections and recommendations of individuals like Henry Hall that Ham Hill Stone came to be used during the Victorian and Edwardian era in many other places beyond its 'sphere of influence'. It became very fashionable in Exeter once supplies could be more easily obtained. The earliest example appears to be No. 4 Cathedral Yard (Edward Ashworth, 1860-64) where it was used at ground floor level with finely jointed red brickwork. It was then used in Sir George Gilbert Scott's restoration of the Cathedral (1870-77) but only for the moulded base for the stairs of the organ loft.[4] More examples would follow: Crown Court Lodge, Castle Street; St Loyes' Foundation, Topsham Road; Wynards Almshouses, Magdalene Street (R. Medley Fulford, 1894) and The Rectory (now a nursing home), Old Tiverton Road; and for the restoration of the 15th-century St Catherine's Almshouse and Chapel when it

Ham Hill Stone was often used with local stones for church restorations in Devon, as here at St Andrew, Halberton: east end with blocks of stone that have remained uncarved.

159

Henry Wilson's Romanesque chancel at St Mary, Lynton, Devon (c.1905).

house was given a new rusticated Hamstone façade in the 19th century.[5] Hamstone dressings were used (with Hurdwick Stone) for the Tavistock UDC's offices in Drake Street of 1900 (now the offices of the Town Council) and for a loosely Edwardian Baroque building in North Street with local stones and a rather ugly red brick. But best of all is Kingdon House, North Street, 'a remarkable Arts and Crafts building by Southcombe Parker *c.*1906. An ingenious treatment of the ground floor to fit the sloping site'.[6] Just outside the town, set back from the Okehampton Road, stands Kelly College (founded in 1867 by Admiral Kelly), an impressive neo-Gothic pile of 1872-4 by C. F. Hanson extended to the east in 1900. It is in Hurdwick Stone with Hamstone dressings.[7] Mount House School, on the Princeton road, is a Georgian brick building but its lodge is Victorian and uses Hamstone dressings with Hurdwick Stone.

Ilfracombe is built mainly of locally quarried sandstones and of a good, if unattractive, yellow Marland brick from near Torrington. Imported stone is mainly Bath Stone. It is therefore a surprise to encounter – to the shrieking of seagulls – the little Catholic church of Our Lady Star of the Sea in Runnacleave Road (1893). Its Hamstone dressings are of an unusually bright gold colour. The former Central Rechabite Hall of 1905 in nearby Northfield Road also has Hamstone dressings. Its chequered career includes the use of its upper floor as a Picture Hall and it is now being converted for use as flats.

Churches

A great deal of Ham Hill Stone was used in Devon generally, including buildings of some prestige. It became very popular amongst architects and their clients for new churches and church restorations throughout the county, even in the 'far west', though most are in east Devon as would be expected from the fact that Ham Hill's 'sphere of influence' had long included much of this part of Devon. An interesting example is Halberton, just east of Tiverton, where Ham Hill Stone was used for new battlemented parapets and hunky-punks in the restoration (1847-9) of the 14th-century St Andrew's church containing mostly red sandstone and Beer Stone. It is all done in a most convincing medieval manner; the architect, John Hayward, had clearly seen other medieval churches in east Devon (such as

Calstock and Stockland) where Hamstone had been used in this fashion in the original churches. An odd detail at Halberton is the pair of projecting Hamstone blocks at parapet level at the east end of the church, clearly intended to be carved into hunky-punks but for some reason abandoned. North Devon has the unusual church of St Mary, the parish church of Lynton and Lynmouth, a blend of medieval and Art Nouveau,

Sidbury Manor, Sidbury, Devon (1879, David Brandon): red brick with Hamstone dressings.

for it was restored between 1893 and 1905 by the architect J. D. Sedding and, after his death, Henry Wilson. It has rubble walls but the dressings are mostly Hamstone. The architect G. E. Street was engaged in 1861 to design the church of St John the Evangelist, Torquay on an imposing site overlooking the harbour and bay, using local stone with heavy details and dressings in Ham Hill Stone. Not far away Edward Appleton built an extension to Torre Abbey in a Tudor style with Hamstone windows. And from the end of our present period, a 'real' Abbey was built between 1907 and 1937 to the designs of an architect, Frederick Walters, but by the labour of the brothers, one of whom had trained as a mason for the purpose. This was Buckfast Abbey, Buckfastleigh, on the southern fringe of Dartmoor, where a Norman Abbey had been founded centuries before but had all but disappeared. The style of the new buildings was Romanesque (with some Transitional details) as part of the monastery's bold quest to re-create what had been destroyed. Though built entirely in the 20th century, in spirit and style it belongs to the age of 19th-century Revivalism. The building stones that were used in the Abbey church are described in the following terms by the brothers who wrote the first guidebook to the new Abbey:

Externally it consists of a hard local limestone, varying in colour from grey to purple, with freestone work

Sidbury Manor: detail of some of the carving of the high-quality stone used in this stylistically eclectic building.

Knightshayes, near Tiverton, Devon (1869-79, William Burges): Hensley Sandstone with abundant Hamstone dressings.

in Giting [sic], and Ham Hill stone of a raw sienna colour from Somerset quarries. The interior is cream Bath stone and the vaulting of Devonshire red sandstone.[8]

Country Houses

Two very different Victorian architects selected Ham Hill Stone for two very different country houses in east Devon. The first was William Burges (1827-81), a 'High Victorian' best known for his work for the Marquis of Bute at Cardiff Castle and Castell Coch, who was employed by John Heathcote-Amery to build Knightshayes Court (1869-79), now a property of the National Trust, on a site looking down from the north towards Tiverton and the family silk mills. The main house, lodge and stables are all Gothic and built of local red Hensley sandstone with Ham Hill Stone splashed about freely for the dressings and for carved details. The colour contrast is not ideal but the effect is certainly memorable. The other was David Brandon who was engaged at Sidbury Manor, near Sidmouth, also completed in 1879 in a riot of Jacobean and French Château styles in red brick with Hamstone quoins, window dressings and very fine carved details. Whoever selected the stone for Brandon knew his job, as it is of a higher quality than much that was coming out of the quarries at that time. The stone continued to be used on the estate post-Brandon for a number of lodges, houses and service buildings, some designed by the proprietor Walter Cave, himself an architect, mainly in the Arts and Crafts idiom. Another country house in which the stone was used is Harcombe House, Chudleigh.

164

CORNWALL

Cornwall is a county surprisingly rich in building stones. They include some sandstones but they are mainly granite and other igneous stones. Liskeard, for example, contains several buildings that demonstrate well that subtle, even quite delicate, effects can be achieved by a blend of stones from the local igneous rocks. So there would seem to be no need to import Ham Hill Stone into the county at all, however good the rail connections became. Yet it can still be found here and there: in St Austell, for example, in an extension to the parish church by the architect J. P. St Aubyn in 1885-6 and in Launceston where it features in the Liberal Club, Northgate Street (1897) as well as in two large but undistinguished buildings, one at the corner of Broad Street and Western Road and the other at the corner of Church Street and Northgate Street (overlooking, incidentally, the remarkable display of granite carving in the parish church). When other buildings in this attractive town show how local stones can be used to such interesting effect, it is a puzzle why Ham Hill Stone should have been used at all here and in such an uninspiring way.

Cornwall's most important 19th-century building is Truro Cathedral, built between 1880 and 1903 and the first cathedral since Salisbury to be built on a new site. Its distinguished architect, J. L. Pearson, was clearly inspired by Salisbury Cathedral in many of the motifs he employs but, with the benefit of his 19th-century perspective, he has created a Gothic cathedral that avoids many of the design weaknesses of the 13th-century structure.[9] It is made largely of Mabe granite with carved exterior details of Bath Stone (Box Ground) and some Doulting Stone. The theme of granite and the pale Bath limestone is continued inside but with variety provided by a dozen or more other types of stone. Among these is Ham Hill Stone, which has been used for the shafts of the pillars in the blind arcades around the walls of the chapels at the east end.

Further west is J. D. Sedding's All Saints Church, Killigrew Street, Falmouth (1887-90). According to the official listing it is built of Great Plymouth Stone with Doulting and Hamstone dressings, although none of the latter could be found.

DORSET

In addition to the large number of 19th-century church restorations that one would expect to find in Dorset – especially in the western part of the county – there are a number of buildings of distinction in which Ham Hill Stone has been used. At Rampisham the former Rectory of 1845-7 (later *Glebe Farm* and now *Pugin Hall*) is by Augustus Welby Pugin – 'a fine design, and in its sensitive vernacular style as progressive as Butterfield's Coalpitheath parsonage [near Bristol] of the same year'.[10] Pugin Hall is unusual in having two personalities: its two most prominent façades are all 'vernacular' but its more intimate east side contains the pointed windows contains similar materials with chamfered Hamstone quoins. We have just seen how Blomfield would later be undertaking a great deal of work at Sherborne, and there is the possibility that he was already familiar with the area and, like Henry Hall before him (in relation to Salisbury), he was anxious to use a stone at Medmenham that he had come to admire in its local area. And Ham Hill Stone even reached the distinguished environs of Cambridge at the turn of the century. At Trinity Hall, the Master's Lodge had been rebuilt by Salvin in 1852 but was 'given its present form'[15] in 1890 by Grayson & Ould, architects of Chester. It is in Tudor style with a Hamstone façade and a castellated parapet in a lighter grey stone. They went on to design the Latham building nearby in Elizabethan style in red brick but with much Ham Hill Stone in the dressings and the prominent bay windows. Also of this time is Westcott House, Jesus Lane – a theological college with 'a friendly Tudor brick court-yard'.[16] Perhaps its Hamstone dressings and carvings contribute to the friendly atmosphere.

In Essex there is even an example of a Hamstone building of this era that has come and gone. Easton Lodge was built at Little Easton (near Great Dunmow) in 1902 to the design of Harold Peto, but it had been demolished by the 1930s and much of its fabric dispersed and incorporated in other houses being built in the locality. The garden, however, with many of its Hamstone features – ponds, balustrades, urns, even a Classical pavilion – has survived.

Southampton's principal Roman Catholic church, St Edmund's, was opened in 1889 and built in Decorated Gothic style to the design of J. W. Lunn. It is of red brick with stone dressings. These are all of Ham Hill Stone, except, for some reason, the most striking feature of the church, the rose window at the 'west' end (facing east towards The Avenue on which the church stands), which is of Bath Stone and 'reputed to be one of the finest in England'.[17] Its ten Hamstone clerestory windows contain elaborate flowing tracery, each window being different. The design also included a tower, 180 feet high, of which the upper storeys were to be built of Ham Hill Stone. This would have been an unusual sight, so far from 'Hamstone country', but the tower was not included in the initial contract and has never been built.

WALES

There is even an example outside England from this period, namely, the Unitarian Church in West Grove, Cardiff (E. H. Bruton, 1886). The walls are of red brick but such is the scale of the usage of Ham Hill Stone in the Italianate design that, on its street frontage, the area of stonework exceeds that of the brick. Not only are the heavy window dressings, cornices and plat bands of stone, but it has been used for the belvedere-like belfry, the roof top pediment (a feature that saves the building from looking more like a gentleman's club than a church), the elaborate porch, the massive corner pilasters and the deep plinth. The intention must have been that, if this fashionable stone was to be brought this far (when there were so many other good stones nearer to hand), it would be used in a way that could not possibly be missed. One possible explanation for the use of the stone is that the founder of the church came from Bridgwater in Somerset.

BANK BUILDINGS

And finally there are the banks. There is an oft-repeated story, although it may be apocryphal, that a West Country bank had taken a quarry at Ham Hill as security for a loan and when the debtor defaulted used the stone for its own bank buildings. One bank that may well have found itself in this situation was the Wilts and Dorset Banking Company, formed in 1835 with its headquarters in Salisbury's Market Place. We have already seen how a new, more prestigious, building was built there in 1869. Now, in 1878 the company built a new bank (of Ham Hill Stone) in Old Christchurch Road, Bournemouth. The builders were Messrs. George & Harding of Bournemouth, who had been founded in 1867 and are still in business there. Colin Harding (great-grandson of the co-founder) says that the story in his family had been that the company specified stone from Ham Hill for its buildings because of its ownership of a quarry there as mortgagees. (The company's successors, Lloyds TSB, are unable to say why the stone was used.) Even assuming this explanation is correct, it would only apply to Hamstone bank buildings in Wiltshire and Dorset (and perhaps a few in Hampshire and Surrey, where the company is believed to have had branches e.g. at Bournemouth, Lymington and Guildford). It is unlikely to account for those in Somerset, Devon or Oxfordshire. Moreover, many of them are now used by NatWest Bank (rather than Lloyds TSB) and a few by the other major banks. It is quite plausible that, as more quarry proprietors got into financial difficulties at the end of the century, there was more than one bank that found itself the owner of a stone quarry. On the other hand, the more likely explanation is that Ham Hill Stone became established as the stone in the region that best gave out the impression of quality and prestige that bank buildings were meant to have.

There are certainly many of them in the West Country; the small towns of Axminster, Glastonbury and Ilminster, for example, each have two. Nearly all have been entirely faced in Ham Hill Stone, usually in a suitably respectable Classical style or (as in Salisbury) in the style of an imposing Italian *palazzo*.

NatWest Bank, Crewkerne (1838): the earliest of the many Hamstone banks throughout southern England.

themselves would have come from the freemasons' yard as uniform and as smooth as possible with any irregularities taken care of later by smoothing the entire façade with a comb-like tool called a drag. These techniques would, no doubt, have been used for Hamstone ashlar façades in places like Yeovil, Crewkerne and Ilminster. They were hardly new techniques, of course, as Bishop Roger's 12th-century ashlar work at Sherborne Castle and the stone façades of late Gothic Hamstone churches such as at Norton-sub-Hamdon will testify.

But the normal use of lime putty is to make mortar by mixing it with sand and water (for ordinary stone or brickwork) and, in addition, with gravel for 'tougher jobs' such as filling the cavities in the rubble infill of a large column or thick wall. It is also the basic ingredient for external renders and internal plasterwork as well as lime washes used for both decoration and protection. In whatever form the slaked lime is used, the intention is that in due time the putty itself or the mix of which it is a constituent will 'set' and gradually take on the characteristics of limestone. This is the process that closes what is sometimes called the lime cycle, the conversion of the slaked lime $(Ca(OH)_2)$ to a state equivalent to that of the limestone whence it was derived $(CaCO_3)$. This occurs by the dual process of slowly losing its water content (H_2O) and absorbing carbon dioxide (CO_2) from the atmosphere. Like the slaking process this will take time. Whereas modern mortars normally set hard overnight, the mark of a successful lime-based mortar is that it remains flexible and never truly 'hardens' at all. Similarly, modern paints often dry within a few hours whereas it is advisable to allow five days between coats of limewash even in warm dry conditions.[1]

So what is wrong then with Portland cement, which is cheaper and easier to use and hardens very quickly? In brief, it is too hard and too impermeable and in a building designed to move and breathe its use can lead to serious problems. Lime mortar is more flexible than the stone around it and so can yield to pressures brought about by settlement and movement. Somerset's great Perpendicular church towers could not have stood for centuries in the English weather without this yielding characteristic of lime-based cements and mortars (plus timely and proper maintenance). The walls of many older Hamstone houses have no cavities and rely on lime mortar and internal renders to be able to breathe. It is the permeability of the stone and the mortar that keeps them dry! Dampness is kept out by the thickness of the walls. Any dampness that gets through is soon drawn up through the fire flue. Portland cement renders or modern paints with low permeability will trap water in the walls. This has to come out through the stone (rather than through the mortar) and can lead to crumbling and decay. The hazards are spelt out in alarming terms in *Lime*, a guide to the use of lime in historic buildings written by Alison Henry for South Somerset District Council:

Further damage is caused by rainwater seeping into the cracks in the pointing and around the edges of the stones. Because the mortar is not permeable this moisture cannot evaporate from the mortar joint once rain stops. Instead it is forced to evaporate through the face of the brick or stone and soluble salts present in the water crystallise in the surface layers of the masonry leading to crumbling and decay. This is sometimes so severe that the entire face of the stone is lost and the hard cement pointing is left standing proud. Further rainwater is trapped and the decay continues. The concentration of trapped water in the masonry also increases its susceptibility to frost damage in the winter.[2]

This is exactly what has occurred to the tower of St. Michael's church on top of Glastonbury Tor. In 1948 the Ministry of Works, as part of a well-intentioned renovation, re-pointed the walls with cement mortar.[3] Apart from the gloomy appearance that this gave the building, the effect on the medieval stonework had, by the end of the century, become a matter of concern to its current managers, the National Trust. In 2003, the cement mortar was replaced by lime mortar with benefits both for the appearance and the future preservation of the building. Similarly, it has been necessary to remove a good deal of cement mortar from the tower of St. Mary, Beaminster as part of its recent restoration.

The Romans were certainly not the inventors of lime production but they undertook it on a huge scale. The only written source we have for Roman practice is the *Ten Books on Architecture* written by Vitruvius in the 1st century AD. In Book I, after advising on sand – which are the best types for different kinds of jobs – he suggests (in Chapter V) that lime should be burnt from stone that is 'white' and that lime made from close-grained stone 'of the harder sort' is best in the structural parts but lime of porous stone in stucco. His recommended mixes for mortar are 3:1 with lime for pitsand and 2:1 with lime for river or sea-sand, preferably, in the latter case, mixed with 'a third part' of burnt brick pounded up and sifted. This is because Vitruvius regarded these as 'thinner' and the brick would help to bulk them up. He then displays a bent for natural philosophy by speculating about the nature of lime:

> The reason why lime makes a solid structure on being combined with water and sand seems to be this: that rocks, like all other bodies are composed of the four elements. Those which contain a large proportion of air are soft; of water, are tough from the moisture; of earth, hard; and of fire, more brittle. Therefore, if limestone, without being burnt, is merely pounded up small and then mixed with sand and so put into the work, the mass does not solidify nor can it hold together. But if the stone is first thrown into the kiln, it loses its former property of solidity by exposure to the great heat of the fire, and so with its strength burnt out and exhausted it is left with its pores open and empty. Hence, the moisture and air in the body of the stone being burnt out and set free, and only a residuum of heat

being left lying in it, if the stone is then immersed in water, the moisture, before the water can feel the influence of the fire, makes its way into the open pores; then the stone begins to get hot, and finally, after it cools off, the heat is rejected from the body of the lime.

Consequently, limestone when taken out of the kiln cannot be as heavy as when it was thrown in, but on being weighed, though its bulk remains the same as before, it is found to have lost about a third of its weight owing to the boiling out of the water. Therefore its pores being thus opened and its texture rendered loose, it readily mixes with sand, and hence the two materials cohere as they dry, unite with the rubble, and make a solid structure.[4]

A modern-day chemist might not wish to quarrel too much with this!

Andrea Palladio is perhaps the best known of the architects and writers of the Renaissance who based their own approach to building practice and design on Roman precedent. His *Four Books of Architecture* would prove to be very influential in England in the 17th and 18th centuries. In this work he frequently acknowledges his respect for what Vitruvius had to say and the practical advice he offers both on sand and lime is not materially different from that of Vitruvius; he does also suggest, however, that 'pebbles found in rivers and rapid streams, are excellent for lime, and make very white neat work'.[5] Calcination, he says, generally takes 60 hours, after which he advises slaking by adding the water in easy stages, then leaving in a moist shady place, covering lightly with sand and taking care not to mix anything with it. When used for making mortar, it should be mixed well with the sand. (Book I Chapters IV and V.)

The Renaissance is often regarded as the great revival of 'ancient' wisdom after centuries of neglect but this is certainly an over-simplification in relation to building techniques. The most obvious early source of continuity was Byzantium. And then a great deal of scientific and technical knowledge came from the Arabs, who had inherited not only much of the accumulated wisdom of the early cultures of the Middle East but also a great deal from Greece. And finally (coming closer to home) the collapse of Roman rule was hardly the reversion to barbarism it was once portrayed to be: most regions of the empire developed their own cultures and technologies but absorbed and kept alive many Roman practices in doing so.[6] At any rate, lime continued to be used throughout the Middle Ages and it can hardly be said that the builders of the Gothic churches and cathedrals from the 12th century onwards needed a Vitruvius to come along and guide them. (His *Ten Books* were only important in the context of the revival of the Classical architecture of Rome.) The following extract of a work from the 9th century is revealing, not only for its mention of 'seething' lime, but for the vision it affords us of the religious spirit that imbued the building of churches. It comes from *Liber Officialis*, a work highly regarded throughout the Middle Ages, written in 823 by Amalar of Metz, and dedicated to the Emperor Louis the Pious.

> When we come together to pray to God, it is appropriate for us to know that we must have the work of building the walls for our church, like those the city of Jerusalem had. ... The walls of our church are founded in Christ. On his foundation are fixed the Apostles and as they through this believed, so do we believe. We are putting these walls together now, and they will continue to be built up until the end of the world. Each and every one of the Saints whom God has ordained to eternal life is a stone in these walls. One stone is laid on top of the next when the teachers of the church train disciples to study, to teach, to improve and to strengthen the holy church. Each one has above him a stone that bears a brotherly load. ... The bigger stones, both the smoothed ones and the hewn blocks, which (as an outer skin) are placed in front on both sides, in whose middle the smaller stones lie, are the more perfect men who preserve the weaker pupils or brothers in the holy church through their exhortations and prayers. The walls cannot be strong without mortar; mortar is made from the lime, sand and water. The seething lime is the love, which combines with the sand. ... But to make lime and sand suitable for use in building a wall, they have to be mixed with water. Water is the Holy Ghost. ... For in the same way that the stones in a wall cannot be linked together without mortar, nor can people be brought together in the building of the New Jerusalem without the love of the Holy Ghost.[7]

No room, then, for Portland cement in the building of the New Jerusalem. (And it would take 1001 years from the writing of these words before it was patented!) What was required was the 'love' of the seething lime, and this near-magical substance would continue to be used until modern times. This is why, although it may have only a limited role in modern building construction, its use remains as important as ever in the repair and maintenance of older buildings. Various interested parties came together a few years ago to form the Building Limes Forum in order to study the material in more depth. And in the last decade there has been a dramatic increase in research into the properties of lime-based mortars, usually for conservation applications.[8] Despite recent advances there is still a great deal more to learn and many more building practitioners to be converted and trained. Yet an interesting development is that as more building practitioners become aware of the advantages of lime they are beginning to use it in new buildings where some movement or settlement can be expected – especially modern timber-framed buildings. 'Once craftsmen builders have been introduced to the working qualities and appearance of lime mortars there is usually no turning back.'[9]

To make one's own lime putty is not recommended unless you know exactly what you are doing[10] but many lime products are now more readily available and being more widely used. Within the 'Hamstone country', for

Castle Street, Bridgwater: some of the splendid local brick with Hamstone dressings.

example, a range of such products is available from Limebase Products Ltd. of Isle Brewers, Somerset and from Rose of Jericho Ltd. of Holywell, Dorset. Also, the country's only manufacturer of 'hydraulic' lime, Hydraulic Lias Limes Ltd., is currently based in Somerset. This is at Trout Quarry, Charlton Adam where the local Blue Lias is particularly suitable – on account of its relatively high content of alumina, silica and iron oxide – for producing this special type of lime mortar capable of setting under water. However, the company has been unsuccessful in obtaining planning permission either for the continued use of its present site beyond September 2005 or for an alternative site in Somerset. It plans to re-establish its business in another part of England's Jurassic limestone belt. It is doubtful whether building lime has been produced at Ham Hill itself for at least a hundred years but Ham Hill Stone Co. Ltd., the proprietors of the southern quarry, are contemplating manufacturing it once again. It would be a great advantage to be able use lime products made from Ham Hill Stone in conjunction with the use of the stone itself – both for lime mortar in walls and, more especially, for 'plastic repairs' discussed in Chapter 15.

Lime mortar is also the traditional material for binding bricks together and a few words on bricks may not be out of place. With such a wealth and variety of building stones in the region it might be thought that brick has been rarely used. This is certainly not a part of the country in which the use of brick was introduced early (as in East Anglia): a little, perhaps, in the 17th century but most of what we see today is from the 18th century onwards. Parts of the Somerset Levels did not enjoy a local source of building stone and bricks were made either from local sources of suitable clay or, increasingly, by the brick industry centred in Bridgwater. In Bridgwater itself, the elegant Georgian terraces of Castle Street are of a fine local brick (some of the buildings with Hamstone quoins) as are those in the uncompleted King Square. Taunton's central building, its Market House designed by the 'gentleman architect', C. W. Bampfylde of Hestercombe, in 1770, is also of brick. By the 19th century the brick business had positively exploded and Brian Murless in his *Somerset Brick and Tile Manufacturers, a brief history and gazetteer* is able to list 264 manufacturers that operated during the 19th or early 20th centuries in every corner of Somerset including many in the Yeovil area.[11] Thomas, too, refers surprisingly often to former sources of local brick in west Dorset, usually where Oxford Clay was present.[12] There is a great deal of brick in the 'Hamstone country', often in buildings with Hamstone quoins and dressings. But the blend is rarely a happy one in visual terms – especially when the brick is red, which is normally the case.

Former Boots chemist shop, Salisbury, Wiltshire (1928): brick with Hamstone dressings.

Lutyens, C. F. A. Voysey and others, would continue to influence house-building in England for many years yet. It was rather the widespread national desire for progress and modernity of the late 1950s and 1960s, as well as great technological advance in the 1970s, that brought about the greatest changes. This was a matter of meeting new needs by a new way of building but it soon led to the neglect of traditional methods and skills. Far more significantly, there seemed to prevail a general amnesia about the country's architectural heritage and a lack of concern about the impact of new development on the old. But gradually the pendulum has swung – some would say too far – in favour of conservation. On the one hand stand those who believe that so much has been lost that we cannot afford to lose or alter what remains. On the other are those who argue that some conservation is all very well but it should not be allowed to stand in the way of legitimate current needs. Every day, it seems, there is a new battle to be fought and another difficult judgment to be made.

So it is not surprising that the demand for building stone has undergone a great change. We saw in Chapter 4 how the quarries at Ham Hill declined and finally closed altogether before a revival in the last twenty years or so. This will be reflected in the examples of Hamstone usage that follow: some intermittent usage during the first sixty years or so after the end of World War I but a steadier usage in recent years. Whilst there is no attempt here to look at stone quarrying as a whole, there has clearly been a drastic

Former Gaumont cinema, Taunton (1931-2, W.T. Beslyn): Hamstone columns and window surrounds.

decline, probably starting early in the 19th century, in the number of the small local quarries that were such an important part of local building practice in 'stone areas'. The significance of this for Ham Hill Stone will be considered in due course.

For an example of development between the wars, we start with Salisbury, as in the last chapter. In 1928, Boots Cash Chemists of Nottingham built one of their new popular stores on a prominent corner site in the High Street to the design of its own architects' office. It was a conservative design, being a modern interpretation of the Classical style. The building has red brick on the first floor with Hamstone dressings and ornamental features and more of both on the ground floor with green Westmorland slate around the windows (which, remarkably, have survived). For once the mixture of Ham Hill Stone and red brick works quite well, the bricks being of a mellow shade and of high quality. This was the last complete building in Salisbury that would see the use of Ham Hill Stone, though some is still needed from time to time for repairs and restoration. Taunton's contribution to this era is rather livelier – the former Gaumont cinema in Corporation Street (now a Bingo Hall), one of England's foremost cinema buildings built in 1931-2 to an Art Deco design of W. T. Beslyn. Its walls are of brick enlivened by well-crafted geometrical designs, but a row of rectangular Hamstone columns stands at its entrance and the

189

In 1938, the stone was used for Hamstone House, one of the best of the mansions on the leafy St George's Hill Estate, Weybridge in Surrey – both in the main house and in its lodge. It is likely that this was the last significant supply of the stone before the quarries closed – not to re-open for about 40 years. It is an interesting building, designed by Ian Forbes, with which to bring an era to a close: ashlar-faced, simple Classical lines and some good carved details.

Any use of the stone within the 'Hamstone country' between the wars appears to have been on a modest scale. There are no major buildings that one can point to, but houses built in local villages by the local authority or the Duchy of Cornwall Estate were either of Hamstone rubble or brick with Hamstone quoins. In the period immediately after World War II no stone was available (and would, perhaps, have been seen as an unnecessary luxury if it were); thus many houses in West Chinnock, for example, stand out for having been built in a poor quality brick. In a bigger place like Yeovil the contrast with older stone buildings is not so evident since the modern estates of brick or render are visually separated from the older town centre. The absence of new supplies of Ham Hill Stone no doubt also explains how Cotswold Stone came to be used for the Medlycott Building in the Great Court of Sherborne School (O. S. Breakspear, 1954-5) rather than a more local stone, though enough Ham Hill Stone was apparently located for the dressings of the porch. During the 1960s and '70s in particular, many houses were built of artificial stone loosely resembling Ham Hill Stone. Some of these appear as what they are – artificial, but many of them are quite acceptable, more so than some built today with 'natural stone' facings.[2]

Following the full re-opening of the quarries in 1982, the situation is changing. At the same time there has been a growing awareness of good conservation practice and the need for new development to harmonise with the old. In South Somerset, for example, it has become the accepted practice for local communities to influence the form that new development takes by drafting their own Village Design Statements. Assuming a Statement is acceptable to the District Council, it is then adopted by the Council as formal Supplementary Planning Guidance – supplementary, that is, to the Local Plan for the District. The Statement published for Norton-sub-Hamdon, for example, in 1999 contains an appraisal of the village as it is today, with warts and all, and sets out some practical guidelines for avoiding repetition of past errors and for taking opportunities as they arise to enhance the environment of the village. So far as new development is concerned, it sets out 27 different points of guidance all aimed at maintaining the traditional style and appearance of the village and its buildings. The first two are of special interest here:

Use materials, style and proportions sympathetic to the old village, though not necessarily in exact imitation of it.

Use Hamstone as far as possible, (always for elevations visible from the road) and locally familiar materials for roofs such as pantiles, roman tiles, and slate.

The Tintinhull Village Design Statement (1997) emphasises the need to respect the characteristics of the existing village and its buildings. Its guidelines on building materials are as follows:

Local natural Hamstone should be used, particularly in the Conservation Area.

Clay roof tiles should generally be used. Thatch and slate may be appropriate in certain circumstances.

Whereas Norton and Tintinhull are Hamstone villages, Long Load lies within Blue Lias country but with its southern end touching the 'Hamstone country'. Thus the buildings of Long Load are more varied as regards their materials and this is duly reflected in its Village Design Statement. One of its stated aims is that 'any new construction should be in harmony with existing buildings' and to this end 'where possible' local natural materials should be used and house extensions should be built from materials that match the existing property. The District Council's own design guide (*The Design of Residential Areas*) covers a wide range of issues and deals with materials only briefly and in general terms. Thus, in the context of 'local distinctiveness', it merely advises 'use appropriate materials and follow traditions of local character regions' and 'use regional building forms and materials'. For walls of new dwellings 'use stone wherever possible'.

Similar considerations apply in West Dorset, where the emphasis in the District Council's design guidance is on the use of materials that will be 'appropriate to the area and sympathetic to the natural and built surroundings' and on general design that is 'in harmony with the adjoining buildings and the area as a whole'. Village Design Statements are being produced in West Dorset as well. Most give a good account of the materials that have been used in the village, giving it its present character, and all contain the notion of new buildings needing to be sympathetically integrated into the existing village. However, the first of them to be produced (Bradford Peverell in 2000) makes a more specific and significant recommendation that will be mentioned later.

There is no doubt that building practice has appreciably changed as a result of these policies though there are still a number of problems that need to be faced. We have seen that 'local stone' used to mean just that – stone taken from a quarry within a few miles of the building site. But those

193

Middlemarsh Street. The first is the 'landmark' tower by a roundabout on the Dorchester Road comprising the Fleur de Lis retirement homes, where the stone is used for a high plinth and in the dressings to the brick building attached to the tower. In the heart of the village is a market square with a large and sturdy market house ('Brownsword') raised on bulbous stone columns and with rendered walls and extensive Hamstone dressings.

It is good to see that the Quedam shopping centre in Yeovil, developed about fifteen years ago (illustrated on p. 87), contains some Ham Hill Stone but not too much; Yeovil has taken advantage of the stone over the years but its buildings contain a wide variety of materials. Similarly, the striking modern extension to the redundant church in Bond Street to form 'The Foyer' has walls of rough blocks of various local

Development at Poundbury, Dorchester: Hamstone plinth and dressings.

stones but with Hamstone dressings in the time-honoured fashion. The town's new Leisure Centre in Brunswick Street is a stylish modern building faced with large rough-hewn blocks of stone from Ham Hill. It is called Goldenstones. A notable new development in Ilminster is Ashcombe Court, built in 2000 as sheltered housing accommodation in a modern Palladian design and incorporating an existing Regency mansion (stucco with

Pilkington Laboratories, Acreman Street, Sherborne (1999-2000, Sir Michael Hopkins): a contemporary yet traditional use of Ham Hill Stone.

Ashcombe Court, Ilminster: the entrance block with 'temple front' in smooth ashlar flanked by rubble-walled wings.

large Hamstone quoins). The entire entrance block – its smooth ashlar walls and all Classical details – has been built in Ham Hill Stone of unusually pale appearance. In the Market Place a new Co-op store close to the Market House, in Classical style and with a Hamstone façade, has been built so as to blend in with its surroundings chromatically and (so far as it is possible in the circumstances) stylistically as well. In Taunton the stone has been used for the archway of the small shopping precinct off Fore Street ('Old Market Centre'); this is most appropriate as it lies between the Hamstone

ashlar faced Royal Bank of Scotland and the 'Accessorize' premises.

An imaginative award-winning development that used Hamstone rubble is the Tower House (2001) on the western outskirts of Crewkerne designed by architect Malcolm McAll. The house is an example of good practical skills of execution as well as design to achieve the round shape of the 'tower' and the well-coursed rubble walls. As McAll himself has often experienced, the necessary level of craftsmanship is still a rare commodity. The critical aspects are the way the wall is built up in layers using rubble stones of varying shapes and sizes – so different from a standard brick –and the composition and

Tower House, East Street, Crewkerne: well-laid rubble complementing good design.

(some in Guiting at a time when the supply of suitable Ham Hill Stone was very limited). Some stone mullions were also beyond repair and were replaced, but in general stonework was gently washed and then 'consolidated' (using a fine limewater spray) or repaired with lime mortar. Similarly, University College School, Hampstead (mentioned above) is undertaking a five-year programme of restoration work that commenced in 2002 and will include both methods. Plastic repairs will be used as far as possible in order to preserve the original features but some have already been replaced where they are deemed to be beyond sensible repair. By contrast, work to Hampshire House, Bayswater, undertaken in 2000 over the course of just a few weeks, involved rectifying past mistakes in the use of cement rendering and repairs, some stone replacement and general consolidation. It was an approach that has made this grand building overlooking Hyde Park appear 'as good as new' without any obvious sign of recent work having been carried out.

Ham Hill Stone varies so much in its colour and general appearance that it is often difficult to achieve a good match. For this reason 'patching', replacing only the worst affected blocks of stone, is rarely successful and it may be necessary for an entire feature to be replaced rather than just pieces of it. The ideal state after repair or restoration is that you cannot tell that anything has been done. Stonemason Tom Monaghan remembers working at St John's Almshouses, Sherborne some years ago when the Council official supervising the job did not at first think he had done anything but later wrote to congratulate him!

It is clear from the very large number of Hamstone buildings that have been built over the last thousand years, and from the great quality and national importance of many of them, that a constant supply of the correct stone will be required for many centuries to come – or at any rate 'for the foreseeable future', interpreted as you wish. More than one owner of a major Hamstone building has expressed concern about the proper future maintenance of his property if Hamstone supplies were ever to dry up. However, the Ham Hill quarries have had no equivalent of Bath (with a massive long-term demand for Bath Stone) or London or the Bournemouth/Poole/Christchurch conurbation (for Portland Stone) so there is still plenty of its stone left. And on the face of it there will not be a problem for the conservation of historic Hamstone buildings in the future. But life is never that straightforward and there are some other important conservation issues to be considered. The quarries lie within a scheduled ancient monument and in a Site of Special Scientific Interest (SSSI). The northern quarry at present obtains its stone from areas that have been worked in the past. There are substantial quantities of stone waiting to be won, but it would only be in the event of consent being granted for new quarries to be opened in this sensitive location that it would continue to operate long into the future. The southern quarries have more land in reserve but the process of obtaining all the necessary approvals will be long and hard. It is also likely to be very costly since it would be normal for full archaeological investigations to be insisted upon, which currently cost about £250,000 per hectare, inevitably adding to the problems of commercial viability. (A geophysical survey was undertaken in 2002 of the land to the east of the present quarry and the presence of a large number of features were detected likely to be Iron Age, Roman and medieval.) The owners already maintain that it would not be viable to operate the quarries for conservation purposes only and that it must be free to provide some stone for new buildings.

It is unlikely that the SSSI designation would present the same problems. Such designations are generally associated with flora and fauna but that for Ham Hill is solely on geological grounds. Geologists already have a reasonable understanding of the strata and their relationship to the Yeovil Sands beneath, and provided English Nature is given full opportunity to study new rock exposures it is difficult to imagine that it could raise any objections to future development of the land for quarrying stone. Nor are environmental issues (noise, traffic and so on), that often bedevil quarrying applications, likely to be serious considerations in relation to development on this remote plateau.

An exciting new development is the manufacture once again of Hamstone roof tiles. They were originally produced at the request of the National Trust and the techniques for making them have been developed at the quarries and validated by the Building Research Establishment. Both Barrington Court and Lytes Cary are in need of roof repairs and the Trust hopes that the quarries will be able to provide new Hamstone tiles where required. The Trust undertook its own tests of the new product before deciding whether it would meet its requirements and has recently placed its first order.

And so what of the future? Present trends should make us optimistic. There is generally an increasing respect for our 'heritage' and greater awareness of the need for the proper use of traditional materials, including natural local stone, in places where anything else would jar and be out of place. What will happen in the longer term we cannot say, except that 'in the long run we are all dead'. It is this particular notion that seemed to inspire the poet T. S. Eliot when he wrote 'East Coker' the second of his *Four Quartets* about the cycle of life. He was aware that one of his ancestors had lived in this Hamstone village before emigrating to America in 1660 and Eliot visited it in 1937. His ashes are here and there is a memorial plaque in the south aisle of the parish church bearing the first and last lines of 'East Coker': 'In my beginning is my end. In my end is my beginning'. But the entire first stanza contains some apt, if solemn, thoughts:

2 Some of the stone may have been used at least four times: in the first cathedral; in the re-modelled and enlarged second cathedral at Old Sarum; and in the graveyard wall of the new cathedral before it was later reduced in height to provide stone for the Close wall.

3 'Conglomerate' is a form of sandstone containing rounded blocks, pebbles or boulders.

4 D. M. Waterman, 'Somersetshire and other Foreign Building Stone in Medieval Ireland', *Ulster Journal of Archaeology*, 33 (1970).

5 'Forest' refers to Wychwood, Oxfordshire; 'Marble' to the fact that some types are capable of taking a polish.

6 Alec Clifton-Taylor and A. S. Ireson, *English Stone Building* (London, 1983), p. 24.

7 Hugh Prudden, *Geology and Landscape of Taunton Deane* (Taunton, 2001), p. 19.

8 An uncharacteristically critical remark by him that can be found in the Introduction to the Dorset volume of *BoE*.

Chapter 6. Around Ham Hill

1 O. H. Creighton points out in an article in *History Today*, 53:4 (April 2003), pp. 12-19 that even Norman castles were often built in low-lying positions for better access to communication and resources and were often overlooked by higher ground.

2 John Collinson, *History & Antiquities of the County of Somerset*, 3 vols (Bath, 1791; reprint Gloucester, 1983), vol. 3, p. 316.

3 One of no less than seven Hamstone buildings belonging to the Trust in this part of Somerset. The others are Montacute House; Treasurer's House, Martock; Lytes Cary; Barrington Court; Tintinhull Garden and the Priest's House, Muchelney.

4 Another that has survived in Somerset is at Bishops Lydiard.

5 See chapter 1, note 5 for the full title of this work.

6 Both Coryate and Jones, as well as Ben Jonson and John Donne, had been members of 'the right worshipful fraternity of Sireniacal Gentlemen', a luncheon club that met on the first Friday of the month at the Mermaid tavern near St Paul's Cathedral (see Michael Leapman, *Inigo* (London, 2003), pp. 119-24).

7 To be historically precise, Martock and Bower Hinton are linked by settlements that once had separate identities, namely, Hurst and Newton.

8 For the purpose of judging relative sizes of settlements, the current number of chargeable properties in parishes for Council Tax purposes is a more reliable guide than census returns. The figures for places mentioned in this chapter are Stoke 918; Norton 307; Chiselborough 144; West and Middle Chinnock 263; East Chinnock 226; Odcombe 341; Montacute 340; Martock 2,007; Crewkerne (with West Crewkerne) 3,348; Yeovil (with Yeovil Without) 16,119 [SSDC Annual Report]. A rough guide to population is to multiply these figures by 2.5.

9 Edward Hutton, *Highways & Byways in Somerset* (London, 1912), p. 258.

10 See note 8 above.

11 Hutton [note 9], p. 240.

12 It appears from p. 242 that he had in mind the Castle Inn and the George Inn. The Mermaid is still there but its 16th-century origins are heavily disguised by 18th-century work.

Chapter 7. Romans, Saxons and Normans

1 Peter Leach, *Roman Somerset* (Wimborne, 2001), pp. 31-2.

2 Leach [note 1], p. 90 and for full details see the Somerset Sites and Monuments Record held by Somerset County Council (Planning Dept) at Taunton.

3 See the Historic Environment Record held at County Hall, Dorchester.

4 R. N. Lucas, *Proceedings of the Dorset Natural History and Archaeological Society* [*PDNHAS*], 96 (1974), pp. 57-8.

5 R. N. Lucas, *PDNHAS*, 102 (1980), pp. 88-90.

6 E. H. Large, *PDNHAS*, 89 (1967), pp. 125-6.

7 John Leach, *Journal of the Sherborne Historical Society*, 1 (1964), pp. 8-13.

8 H. S. L. Dewar, *PDNHAS*, 82 (1960), pp. 86-7; these items had been re-used but indicate an earlier building 'which appears to have been of some pretentiousness'.

9 W. G. Putnam, *PDNHAS*, 93 (1971), pp. 160.

10 W. G. Putnam and Anne Rainey, *PDNHAS*, 94 (1972), pp. 81-6.

11 Leach [note 1], p. 112.

12 Leach [note 1], p. 109.

13 Grahame Farr, *Somerset Harbours* (London, 1954), p. 54.

14 Leach [note 1], p. 115.

15 L. F. Salzman, *Building in England Down To 1540: A Documentary History* (Oxford, 1952), p. 192.

16 J. H. P. Gibb, in his excellent guidebook to Sherborne Abbey, tells us that when the plinth of the north transept was excavated it was found to be Hamstone; his fuller account of excavations undertaken in 1964 and 1973 (The Anglo-Saxon Cathedral at Sherborne, available as a booklet at the Abbey) mentions four other stones ('either indubitably or possibly Saxon') that, after scientific analysis, were found to be Hamstone.

17 *BoE: South & West Somerset* (Harmondsworth, 1958).

18 K. R. Potter (editor), *The Historia Novella by William of Malmesbury* (London, 1955), p. 26.

19 John Chandler, *John Leland's Itinerary, Travels in Tudor England* (Stroud, 1993), p. 420.

20 In *Castles of Britain and Ireland* (Newton Abbot, 1996) Plantagenet Fry suggests that the stonework had been added in the first years of the 12th century.

21 *VCH*, vol. 3, p. 215.

22 R. R. C. Gregory, 'Notes on the Discovery of Cary Castle', *Proceedings of the Somerset Archaeological and Natural History Society*, 36 (1890), pp. 168-74.

23 'ita juste composito ordine lapidum, ut junctura perstringat intuitum, et totam maceriam unum mentiatur esse saxum'. William of Malmesbury, *Gesta Regum Anglorum* V 408. (William Stubbs (editor), *De Gestis Regum Anglorum Libri Quinque; Historiae Novellae Libri Tres*, 2 vols (London, 1887; reprinted London, 1964), vol. 2, p. 484.)

Chapter 8. Medieval and Early Tudor

1 W. G. Hoskins, *The Making of the English Landscape* (London, 1955), p. 155 and see Lyndon F. Cave, *The Smaller English House* (London, 1981), pp. 14, 30 et seq.

2 An excellent example (probably of 13th-century origin) can be seen in Salisbury at the High Street entrance to the Old George Mall.

3 Douglas Knoop and G. P. Jones, *The Mediaeval Mason* (Manchester, 1933; revised 1967), p. 25.

4 L. F. Salzman, *Building in England Down To 1540: A Documentary History* (Oxford,

1952), pp. 24-9.

5 Ibid., pp. 123-4.

6 See p.52 re masons called 'Norton' and 'Stoke'.

7 John Allan, 'A Note on the Building Stones of the Cathedral', in Francis Kelly (ed.), *Medieval Art and Architecture at Exeter Cathedral* (Exeter, 1991), pp. 10-18.

8 David Parsons (ed.), *Stone, Quarrying and Building in England AD 43-1525* (Chichester, 1990), p. 111. The drastic difference in cost at that time between water and land transport is well illustrated by Knoop and Jones [note 3], pp. 45-6: at Vale Royal 35,000 loads of stone were carted (over 3 years) from quarries 4-5 miles away; the quarries were paid £104, the carters £347; but at Rochester Castle 2,290 tons of stone was carried by river from the quarries – it cost £119 and the transport £47 14s.

9 C. M. Gerrard, 'Ham Hill Stone: A medieval distribution pattern from Somerset', *Oxford Journal of Archaeology*, 4:1 (1985), pp. 105-12.

10 Arthur Mee, *The King's England: Dorset* (London, 1939), p. 108.

11 Jo Thomas, 'The Building Stones of Dorset, Part I', *Proceedings of the Dorset Natural History & Archaeological Society*, 114 (1992), p. 161.

12 The Abbot of Forde had become a lessee of a quarry at Ham Hill by 1475 (*VCH*, vol. 3, p. 244).

13 The guidebook for the property states that Prideaux 'may have been assisted by Edward Carter, an architect responsible for buildings in the Middle Temple'.

14 Denis Moriarty (ed.), *Alec Clifton-Taylor's Buildings of Delight* (London, 1986), p. 129.

15 *BoE: South and West Somerset* (Harmondsworth, 1958), p. 249.

16 J. Fowler, *The Stones of Sherborne Abbey* (London, 1938), p. 14.

17 Frederick Treves, *Highways and Byways in Dorset* (London, 1906), p. 311. Treves is more famous, perhaps, as the surgeon who removed Edward VII's appendix and who befriended the 'Elephant Man'.

18 It should not surprise us that in Simon Jenkins' *England's Thousand Best Churches* (London, 1999) Sherborne is one of only eighteen churches to which he awards 'Five Stars'.

19 Edward Hutton, *Highways & Byways in Somerset* (London, 1912), p. 242.

20 *Proceedings of the Somerset Archaeological and Natural History Society*, 56 (1910), p. 46.

21 *BoE: Dorset* (Harmondsworth, 1972), p. 278.

Chapter 9. Medieval and Early Tudor: Churches, Memorials and Crosses

1 The conclusion reached, for example, by C. M. Gerrard, whose study 'Ham Hill Stone: A medieval distribution pattern from Somerset', *Oxford Journal of Archaeology*, 4:1 (1985), pp. 105-12 should be treated as having more to do with mathematical analytical techniques than with Hamstone churches.

2 Hugh Prudden, *Geology and Landscape of Taunton Deane* (Taunton, 2001), chapter 4.

3 Jo Thomas, 'The Lesser-known Building Materials of West Dorset', *Proceedings of the Geologists' Association*, 101 (1990), pp. 299-300.

4 John H. Harvey, 'The Church Towers of Somerset', *Transactions of the Ancient Monuments Society's*, 26 (1982), pp. 157-83.

5 John Betjeman (ed.), *Collins Guide to English Parish Churches* (London, 1958), p. 327.

6 In arriving at his own classification, Wickham acknowledges, at pp. 39-40, the work of Professor Freeman in the middle of the 19th century and that of R. P. Brereton culminating in an article in the *Archaeological Journal* in 1904.

7 As amusingly explained by Denis Moriarty in his *Alec Clifton-Taylor's Buildings of Delight* (London, 1986), pp. 136-7.

8 A. K. Wickham, *Churches of Somerset* (Dawlish, 1952), p. 38.

9 Wickham [note 8] p. 61, referring to a series of articles 'Monumental Effigies in Somerset' by Fryer in *Proceedings of the Somerset Archaeological and Natural History Society*, 61-75 (1915-29).

10 Charles Pooley, *The Old Stone Crosses of Somerset* (London, 1877), p. 5.

Chapter 10. Late Tudor and Jacobean

1 *BoE: Dorset* (Harmondsworth, 1972), p. 360.

2 Ibid., p. 278

3 Ibid., pp. 273-4.

4 Ibid., p. 274.

5 Ibid., p. 81.

6 Ibid.

7 English Heritage Research Transactions, *Stone: Stone Roofing* (2003), p. 46.

8 Malcolm Rogers, *Montacute House* (National Trust guidebook, London, 2000), p. 24.

9 Rogers [note 8], p. 11.

10 A system that led to the glorious carved timber staircases that can be seen at Forde Abbey and Dunster Castle.

11 This is very similar to the way the former highway through the grounds of Wilton House, Wiltshire was diverted in the 18th century to the advantage of the owners. It was all of a piece with the vogue for creating a landscape setting around a great country house, even if this meant dispossessing a few householders (or even a whole settlement as at Milton Abbas) in the process.

12 Thomas Coryate, *Coryat's* [sic] *Crudities* (Glasgow, 1905) vol. 2, p. 310.

13 *BoE: Devon* (London, 1989), p. 815.

14 When the school was rebuilt on another site in 1882, the original school building ('Old Blundells') was converted into apartments.

Chapter 11. Stuart to Regency

1 Hamstone examples from the mid-17th century can be seen at Crewkerne, East Coker, Ilton, Donyatt, Staple Fitzpaine and Hinton St George (all Somerset); West Coker's terrace of almshouses is dated 1718.

2 For a full account see Richard Durman, *Classical Buildings of Wiltshire and Bath* (Bath, 2000).

3 Colin G. Winn, *The Pouletts of Hinton St George* (Stroud, 1995), p. 126.

4 Winn [note 3], p. 127.

5 *BoE: South & West Somerset* (Harmondswoth, 1958), p. 140.

6 Ibid.

7 Gwyn Headley & Wim Meulenkamp, *Follies Grottoes and Garden Buildings* (London, 1999), p. 455.

8 'Images of England' website (see Appendix 1).

9 John Chandler, *John Leland's Itinerary, Travels in Tudor England* (Stroud, 1993), p. 417.

10 According to Leland there had been four parish churches 'within living memory' with the remains of two still standing. (Chandler [note 9], p. 417.)

11 Though it is unlikely that the future Queen Victoria noticed this, on what is said to be her first stay at a hotel, as she was less than a year old.

12 He was, for example, Supreme Magus of the Societas Rosicrusiana in Anglia and founder of the Hermetic Order of the Golden Dawn. He was also suspected of being 'Jack the Ripper'.

13 *BoE: Devon* (London, 1989), p. 810. The building stone is incorrectly described as 'yellow sandstone'.

14 In Michael Hall (ed.), *Gothic Architecture and its Meanings 1550-1830* (Reading, 2002), pp. 73-96.

15 It has no dedication, simply being called 'The Church in the Field, Low Ham'.

16 *BoE: Dorset* (Harmondsworth, 1972), p. 379.

Chapter 12. Victorian and Edwardian Era

1 Roger Dixon and Stefan Muthesius, *Victorian Architecture* (London, 1978), p. 15.

2 For most of its life the building was known as the County Hotel but the older name has recently been restored.

3 Wadham identifies about 120 different building stones from all over Britain and Europe (as well as from other parts of the world) in the buildings of Southampton, but only one is in Ham Hill Stone – at the junction of Oxford Street and Bernard Street – used with a yellow brick. Also, outside his study area, is St Edmund's church (see p. 172).

4 I am grateful to John Allan, Curator of Antiquities, Exeter City Museums and Art Gallery, for this information.

5 *BoE: Devon* (London, 1989), p. 785 suggests 'early' in the century but it must surely be after the railway came in 1859.

6 Ibid.; the building is shown in illustration 174.

7 Ibid., p. 787 suggests they are of Bath Stone, which is true of the interior but not of the exterior.

8 Dom Charles Norris and Dom Robert Nicholl, *Buckfast Abbey: A Pictorial Survey* (Buckfast Abbey). The guidebook is neither dated nor paginated but was probably first published soon after the Abbey was completed in 1937 and the words appear on the third page after the end of the Introductory.

9 E.g. the cramped scale of the nave elevations, the over-use of Purbeck stone and the weak design of the west front – though this does not necessarily make Truro the 'better' cathedral!

10 *BoE: Dorset* (Harmondsworth, 1972), p. 356.

11 As you discover by searching for 'Somerset', 'Ham Hill Stone' and 'Victorian' in the Images of England website operated by English Heritage.

12 The pulling down of the old church and the building of the new one features in Patricia Wendorf's novel *Larksleve* (1985).

13 Hugh Prudden, *Geology and Landscape of Taunton Deane* (Taunton, 2001).

14 *BoE: London 6: Westminster* (New Haven & London, 2003), p. 563.

15 *BoE: Cambridgeshire* (Harmondsworth, 1970), p. 181.

16 Ibid., p. 235.

17 Francis Isherwood, *A Short History of St Edmund's Church* (Southampton, 1969), p. 11.

Chapter 13. Lime, Bricks and Mortar

1 One source of practical advice on the use of such products is a series of articles that can be found on the website at www.thelimecentre.co.uk.

2 Alison Henry, *Lime: A Guide to the Use of Lime in Historic Buildings* (Yeovil, 1999), p. 2.

3 Yet in his Foreword to *The English Heritage Directory of Building Limes* (Shaftesbury, 1997) John Fidler tells us that as early as 1913 the Ministry's Chief Architect commented that 'the deleterious effect of Portland cement on (historic) stonework is becoming more widely known' and set out standards of practice in the use of lime in an appendix to the annual report of the Chief Inspector for Ancient and Historic Buildings. But of course two World Wars had intervened by 1948.

4 From the translation by M. H. Morgan first published by Dover in 1960.

5 From the Isaac Ware version of 1738 republished by Dover in 1965.

6 See, for example, Xavier Barral i Altet, *The Early Middle Ages, from Late Antiquity to AD 1000* (Cologne, 2000).

7 Günther Binding, *High Gothic* (Cologne, 2002), p. 48.

8 John Stewart and others, 'Field and Laboratory Assessment of Lime-based Mortars', *Journal of Architectural Conservation*, 1 (March 2001), p. 7: an article dealing with trials held at Corfe Castle, Dorset.

9 From *The Lime Practitioners Guide*, a pamphlet produced by Limebase Products Ltd, with the assistance of the well-known conservator, Nick Durnan.

10 Henry [note 2], p. 8.

11 Somerset Industrial Archaeological Society Survey No. 13 (2000).

12 Jo Thomas, 'The Lesser-known Building Materials of West Dorset', *Proceedings of the Geologists' Association*, 101 (1990), p. 298.

Chapter 14. Recent Times

1 Salisbury was also being provided with a Gaumont cinema in 1931, but it could not be more different, as the auditorium was built behind the medieval 'Hall of John Hall' that serves as the foyer to the cinema to this day. The Hall was one of only two buildings in Salisbury, outside The Close, built in the Middle Ages with stone façades (of Tisbury Stone).

2 One manufacturer that continues to develop and improve its product is Bradstone; their 'Masonry Block' product line (that comes in a variety of sizes) includes a variety that they call 'Weathered Ham'.

3 Contained in Chapter 11 (Design and Amenity) of the Written Statement to the First Deposit version (January 2000) of the West Dorset Local Plan.

4 Actually, it is three houses: 1-3 Great Field Lane.

Chapter 15. Repair, Conservation and the Future

1 M. H. Port (ed.), *The Houses of Parliament* (New Haven & London, 1976), p. 98.

2 This is the conclusion tentatively reached by Mike Lawrence, proprietor of the southern quarry and stone conservation expert.

However, even for this relatively 'local' area, the figures must be treated with the greatest caution. First, mere numbers of buildings can be misleading in that, for example, three entries for a particular place might relate to three substantial buildings or to three headstones in a churchyard. Second, the figures contain patent oddities: the medieval figure for South Somerset, for example, is clearly too low and is a reflection on the technicalities of the search process. Conversely, some of the 'medieval' cases (including that in Mid Devon) are actually examples of 19th-century work to a church with medieval origins. There is also something badly wrong with Sedgemoor's figures since the River Parrett runs through the middle of the District and a very high proportion of its churches contain stone that is likely to have been transported by river from Ham Hill. These figures may possibly give a broad indication of relative numbers of Hamstone buildings between Districts but even that is dubious.

The *Buildings of England* series of books was created by Sir Nikolaus Pevsner and, to quote the blurb of the current Devon volume, 'is an unrivalled series of architectural guides covering every English county and all periods from prehistoric times to the present day.' The Devon volume (first published as a single volume in 1989) is an example of a modern edition that updates and extends Pevsner's original volume (or, in Devon's case, two volumes). The series has become an important national institution that constantly draws on local and national expertise to keep it up to date. It has been an invaluable aid in the production of this book. However, the books are essentially architectural guides and one cannot expect a great deal of information about building stones. For example, in its discussion of the church of St. John Evangelist, Torquay, the only mention of building stones concerns the interior ('the clustered shafts of polished Devon marble with bands of differently coloured marble'). The fact that the church was built largely of Ham Hill Stone is not mentioned. Each volume contains at least a short section in the introduction about building stones (and those written by Alec Clifton-Taylor are especially to be valued) but for individual buildings the data is limited and sometimes incorrect; Pevsner himself was clearly very familiar with Ham Hill Stone and often mentions its existence in a building – but equally often does not.

Where they exist, geological guides to building stones in towns (e.g. Bath; Southampton) or to individual buildings (e.g. Truro Cathedral; Sherborne Abbey - though now out of print) are extremely valuable but they are rarely encountered.

We are fortunate to have two recent geologists' surveys to call on, those of Jo Thomas in west Dorset and Hugh Prudden's book on the geology of Taunton Deane (see Bibliography). The first of these shows that, although local stone is generally the first choice of material throughout the area of the study, Ham Hill Stone was used in medieval churches in all but a handful of those surveyed. Prudden's work contains a list (in Appendix G) of 86 parish churches specifying the different building stones that have been used *in walls and buttresses*; it shows that 35 of the 86 churches contained Ham Hill Stone in the main fabric. It is safe to assume that a much higher proportion would have Hamstone quoins and dressings.

of forty feet, are different strata of the fine hard stone, sixteen lying one on another, without any intervening earth. These strata are from one foot to three feet in thickness; the lower weighing a hundred and a quarter by the solid foot. The perpendicular fissures, or what the quarrymen call gullies, are from ten feet to thirty feet apart. Some quarries on the south-east side of the hill have, at a depth of about twenty feet below the surface, a stratum of yellow sand ochre of three feet thickness. [Collinson [above] vol. 2, p. 334 (in relation to Norton).]

1898 – The ground from which the stone for all our old buildings was obtained is on the western side of the hill, and mostly in the parish of Norton. These old workings were only about twenty feet deep in stone, at most, and the heading was of rubble and thin layers of stone. The stone tiles, with which so many of our old buildings are covered were quarried near the surface, over the workable stone, chiefly from the north part of the hill. Instead of the ochre or sand beds of the deep modern quarries, there were here thin layers of hard stone, which were worked to an even thickness by a tile-pick. The working of tiles is now a lost art on the hill. [Charles Trask, *Norton-sub-Hamdon in the county of Somerset: notes on the parish and the manor and on Ham Hill* (Taunton, 1898), p. 217.]

1898 – The quarrying of the stone, preparatory to removal, is done in much the same way as it was done five hundred years ago. It is cut in grooves with a pick where necessary (the joints being of great assistance in saving this part of the work), and then lifted from its natural bed by wedges driven under it by a sledge hammer. Heavy iron bars are used as levers, and when the stone is raised a few inches, a chain is put under the block, and in a few minutes it is hoisted to the surface by a steam crane. [Trask [above], p.220.]

1910 – The *Ham Hill* (Hamdon) stone occurs as a local calcareous development in the upper part of the Midford Sands [for current definition see p. 61]. … The following may be taken as a representative section of the Ham Hill beds:
'Ochre Beds' (40 feet)
   Sand and thin soft stone
   Sand with thicker beds of stone
Ham Hill Stone
   Main mass of freestone,* indistinctly jointed and false-bedded. Good Stone obtained 7 or 8 feet down, and thence to the bottom in the following sequence (about 50 feet):
     35 feet – Yellow beds (chief part)
         – Coarse bed
     8 feet – Grey beds (most durable)
     6 to 7 feet – Stone beds
Yellow Sands (about 80 feet)
[John Allen Howe, *The Geology of Building Stones* (London, 1910; reprinted Donhead St Mary, 2001), p. 206.]

1932 – Ham Hill stone ... consists of beds of shelly limestone intercalated with seams of clay. On exposure to the weather, the softer seams are eroded more rapidly than the harder, and the stone assumes a characteristic furrowed appearance. In ashlar, provided the stone is laid on its natural bed, this form of weathering is of little importance except in its effect on the appearance of the building, but in projecting or free-standing features, the decay of the softer seams may cause dangerously large masses of stone to fall from the building. But for these faulty seams, Ham Hill stone would possess remarkably good weathering properties. The properties of the shelly portions of the stone appear to be as good as those of the best shelly limestones we have in the country, and it is common to observe in buildings that, except for the erosion of the clay seams, the stone remains practically unharmed by exposure to town atmospheres. [R. J. Schaffer, *The Weathering of Natural Building Stones* (London, 1932), p.11.]

1933 – The famous quarries at Huddleston, Taynton and Barnack were no doubt extensive but some quarries were quite small: the dimensions of a quarry near [*sic*] Ham Hill, Somerset, are given in a lease belonging to the fifteenth century – a period of special activity in that region – as 24 feet square, and according to a sixteenth-century survey of the Parish of Norton, the ancient dimensions of quarries there were 20 feet each way. [Douglas Knoop and G. P. Jones, *The Mediaeval Mason* (Manchester, 1933 revised 1967), pp. 8-9.]

1935 – The Mendips, the Quantocks, Ham Hill, and the hills that lie east of Bath all supplied the medieval builder with the finest stone for architectural purposes; the result is that no county could ever have a more splendid collection of churches, abbeys, and houses to show than Somerset. [Edmund Barber, 'The West Country' in *The Beauty of Britain, a pictorial survey* (London, 1935), p. 50.]

1935 – When the Dissolution came ... the skill of Somersetshire masons and builders added to her treasures in a comparatively short time some of the most interesting and beautiful of country houses. Those who were skilled in the working of Ham Hill stone give us, apart from that matchless jewel Montacute, both Barrington Court and the Tudor front of Brympton d'Evercy. [Barber [above], p. 52.]

1958 – The variety of stones gives the county [Somerset] a colour. Bath quarries provide pale-yellow stone. Doulting stone from which Wells and the Mendip churches are built is silvery-grey; around Somerton and the Polden hills the quarries yield blue lias, which looks particularly good with the old red curly tiles on cottages, and in the west is red sandstone. Finest of all stone is that from Ham Hill in the south. On the Dorset border the old cottages and churches are a rich golden-yellow. [John Betjeman, in his Introduction for Somerset, *Collins Guide to English Parish Churches*, (London, 1958), p.322.]

1962 – [Ham Hill Stone] is one of England's most seductive stones, and places such as Crewkerne, Ilminster, Martock and Montacute owe it an unending debt. It is attractive to lichens, which can give it a mottled appearance, but, far from being a disfigurement, this is usually an asset. Like all iron-tinted stones, it may seem rather to soak up the sunshine than to reflect it back, but in the contemplation of these rich, golden brown surfaces spotted with lichen, usually of freestone* and here and there sumptuously dressed, the eye may find insatiable pleasure. [Alec Clifton-Taylor, *The Pattern of English Building* (London, 1987), p. 88-9.]

1965 - Montacute is built of stone from the local quarry of Ham Hill, which has greatly enriched southern Somerset and the adjacent parts of Dorset. It is a tawny ochre stone which absorbs rather than reflects the sun, and is particularly attractive to lichens which give it a mottled appearance and spread the colour unevenly as if on a painter's palette. It exudes colour like honey, in much the same way as long-weathered Pentelic marble. Equally effective is the use of the same stone inside the house, where it appears creamier, richer and skin-smooth in texture. But the outer walls of Montacute in a setting sun are of such loveliness that if it were the face of a quarry instead of the face of a house, one's pleasure at the sight of it would scarcely be diminished. [Nigel Nicolson, *Great Houses of Britain* (re-published London, 1978 as *The National Trust Book of Great Houses of Britain*), p73.]

1983 - Undoubtedly the most prestigious of these [Liassic] stones is Ham Hill. This used to be regarded as one of the Lower Oolites which it closely resembles; but modern geology has reclassified the stone as belonging to the Upper Lias. Small towns on the Somerset-Dorset border such as Sherborne and Martock, famous houses like Montacute and many churches in the vicinity bear witness to the charm of this seductive golden brown stone, which is due to iron oxide staining. Sometimes, it is true, the iron content causes it to weather very dark and the natural striations within the stone to show conspicuously. [Alec Clifton-Taylor and A. S. Ireson, *English Stone Building* (London, 1983), pp. 21-2.]

1992 - At Ham Hill, near Yeovil, a large mass of shelly limestone of the type present as small lenses or beds elsewhere is known as the 'Ham Hill Stone'. This great lens of shelly debris held together by a ferruginous cement is up to 27m thick and passes laterally into sand with calcareous lenticles. It was extensively quarried at Ham Hill for use as a building stone. [G. W. Green, *British Regional Geography, Bristol and Gloucester region* (London, 1992), p. 105.]

1995 - The Ham Hill Stone is a lens shaped mass of shelly limestones and inter-bedded sands within the rock formation known as the Yeovil Sands. Ammonites ... indicate that the Ham Hill Stone belongs to the Moorei Subzone of the Levesquei Zone (Toarcian Stage). Its age is approximately 170Ma (lower Jurassic Period) ... [H. C. Prudden, *Ham Hill, The Rocks and Quarries* (Yeovil, 1995), p. 8.]

1999 – Ham Stone is a shelly limestone in which all the shells are broken up into small fragments. It appears that it was deposited on shell banks which lay in a north/south belt. These lie in the vicinity of Yeovil, centred on Montacute, where the stone is found today. These fossilised shell banks yield large blocks of yellow ochrous stone which can be carved readily into almost any shape or size. These qualities have established a ready market for the stone throughout the area from early historic times, and it can be seen in almost all the local buildings, whether church or mansion, and even in the humble cottages in the villages. The Ham stone was known to, and used by, the Romans, and is found in buildings of all ages. [Peter Hardy, *The Geology of Somerset* (Bradford-on-Avon, 1999), p. 145.]

2001 – The golden-brown Ham Hill Stone and Guiting Stone are typical of limestones in which iron occurs in the hydrated form of ferric oxide (limonite). [Hugh Prudden, *Geology and Landscape of Taunton Deane* (Taunton, 2001), p. 8.]

2001 – Ham Hill Stone. Yellowish-brown mass of broken shell debris cemented with calcium carbonate and limonite (hydrous oxide of iron); the latter gives the stone its golden colour. The short, sloping beds of irregular thickness are examples of cross-bedding [depositional sedimentary structure with inclined sets of short beds] where weathering has picked out the weaker beds. [Prudden [above], p. 43.]

* For a discussion of whether it is truly a freestone see p. 41.

Public Access to Houses

The following properties (containing Ham Hill Stone) mentioned in the text are open to the public at certain specified times:

National Trust properties

Somerset
Barrington Court
Dunster Castle
Fyne Court
Lytes Cary Manor
Montacute House
Stoke-sub-Hamdon Priory
The Priest's House, Muchelney
The Treasurer's House, Martock
Tintinhull Garden

Devon
Knightshayes Court
Old Blundells, Tiverton (forecourt only)

Other

Somerset
Hestercombe Gardens

Dorset
Minterne Magna House (gardens only but the house may be visited by groups by special arrangement)
Sandford Orcas Manor
Athelhampton House
Mapperton House (gardens only)
Forde Abbey

Devon
Cadhay, Ottery St Mary

All other houses mentioned in the text as containing Ham Hill Stone are in private occupation and may only be visited by express prior arrangement with the owner or occupier.

Bibliography

Books

Malcolm Airs, *The Tudor & Jacobean House, a building history* (Stroud, 1995).

John Ashurst and Francis G. Dimes, *Conservation of Building and Decorative Stone* (Oxford, 1990).

Bath Geological Society, *Bath in Stone, a guide to the city's building stones* (Kingston Bagpuize, 2001).

Tim Beaumont-James, *The Palaces of Medieval England* (London, 1990).

Eric Benfield, *Purbeck Shop, a Stoneworker's Story of Stone* [1940], introduction by Brian R. Bugler (Southampton, 1990).

Norman Bezzant, *Out of the Rock* (London,1980).

Günther Binding, *High Gothic* (Cologne, 2002).

Antony Cartwright, *The Building and Ornamental Stones of Truro Cathedral* (Truro, 1997).

Lyndon F. Cave, *The Smaller English House* (London, 1981).

John Chandler, *John Leland's Itinerary, Travels in Tudor England* (Stroud, 1993).

Bridget Cherry and Nikolaus Pevsner, *The Buildings of England: Devon* (London, 1989).

Alec Clifton-Taylor, *The Pattern of English Building* (London, 1987).

Alec Clifton-Taylor and A. S. Ireson, *English Stone Building* (London, 1983).

John Collinson, *History & Antiquities of the County of Somerset,* 3 vols. (Bath, 1791; reprint Gloucester, 1983).

Howard Colvin (ed.), *History of the King's Works,* 4 vols. (London, 1976-82).

Clare Conybeare, *The King's House, Salisbury: A Short History* (Salisbury, 1987).

Ken Dark, *Britain and the End of the Roman Empire* (Stroud, 2000).

The Devonshire Association, *The Building Stones of Devon* (Bradford-on-Avon, 1992).

Roger Dixon and Stefan Muthesius, *Victorian Architecture* (London, 1978).

Robert Dunning, *Somerset Castles* (Tiverton, 1995).

Robert Dunning, *Somerset Monasteries* (Stroud, 2001).

Grahame Farr, *Somerset Harbours* (London, 1954).

Neil Faulkner, *The Decline and Fall of Roman Britain* (Stroud, 2000).

J. Fowler, *The Stones of Sherborne Abbey* (London, 1938).

G. W. Green, *British Regional Geography, Bristol and Gloucester region* (London, 1992).

Cecil C. Handiside, *Building Materials* (London, 1958).

Peter Hardy, *The Geology of Somerset* (Bradford-on-Avon, 1999).

Donald Hill, *A History of Engineering in Classical and Medieval Times* (London, 1984).

W. G. Hoskins, *The Making of the English Landscape* (London, 1955).

John Allen Howe, *The Geology of Building Stones* (London,1910; reprint Donhead St Mary, 2001).

Kenneth Hudson, *The Fashionable Stone* (Bath, 1971).

Edward Hutton, *Highways & Byways in Somerset* (London, 1912).

Douglas Knoop and G. P. Jones, *The Mediaeval Mason* (Manchester, 1933; revised 1967).

Peter Leach, *Roman Somerset* (Wimborne, 2001).

Elaine Leary, *The Building Limestones of the British Isles* (Building Research Establishment, 1983).

Thomas Maude, *Guided by a Stonemason* (London & New York, 1997).

Denis Moriarty (editor), *Alec Clifton-Taylor's Buildings of Delight* (London, 1986).

Richard Muir, *The Stones of Britain* (London, 1986).

John Newman and Nikolaus Pevsner, *The Buildings of England: Dorset* (Harmondsworth, 1972).

Nikolaus Pevsner, *The Buildings of England: North Somerset and Bristol* (Harmondsworth, 1958).

Nikolaus Pevsner, *The Buildings of England: South and West Somerset* (Harmondsworth, 1958).

David Parsons (editor), *Stone, Quarrying and Building in England AD 43-1525* (Chichester, 1990).

Charles Pooley, *The Old Stone Crosses of Somerset* (London, 1877).

Hugh Prudden, *Geology and Landscape of Taunton Deane* (Taunton, 2001).

H. C. Prudden, *Ham Hill, The Rocks and Quarries* (Yeovil, 1995).

Bill Putnam, *The Romans* (Discover Dorset series) (Wimborne, 2000).

A. V. Richards, *The History of Stoke-sub-Hamdon* (Stoke-sub-Hamdon, 1970; revised 1993).

Peter Rockwell, *The Art of Stoneworking* (Cambridge, 1993).

Malcolm Rogers, *Montacute House* (National Trust guidebook) (London, 2000).

Royal Commission on Historical Monuments (England), *Ham Hill, Somerset: A New Survey by RCHME* (Swindon, 1997).

Royal Commission on Historical Monuments (England), *Salisbury, The Houses of The Close* (London, 1993).

L. F. Salzman, *Building in England Down To 1540, a Documentary History* (Oxford, 1952).

Peter Saunders, *Salisbury in Old Photographs* (Gloucester, 1982).

R. J. Schaffer, *The Weathering of Natural Building Stones* (London, 1932).

Jo Thomas, *Stone Quarrying* (Discover Dorset series) (Wimborne, 1998).

Giorgio Torraca, *Porous Building Materials* (Rome,1988).

Charles Trask, *Norton-sub-Hamdon in the county of Somerset: notes on the parish and the manor and on Ham Hill* (Taunton, 1898).

Victoria History of the County of Somerset: 8 vols. [in progress] (London, 1906-2004).

Anthony Wadham, *Building Stones of Southampton, Four Geological Walks around the City Centre* (Southampton, n.d.).

John Watson, *Building Stones* (Cambridge, 1911).

A. K. Wickham, *Churches of Somerset* (Dawlish,1952; revised London, 1964).

V. Wilson and others, *Geology of the Country around Bridport and Yeovil (Memoirs of the Geological Survey of Great Britain)* (London, 1958).

Colin G. Winn, *The Pouletts of Hinton St George* (Stroud, 1995).

Articles, Advisory Notes and Unpublished Material

John Allan, 'A Note on the Building Stones of the Cathedral', in Francis Kelly (editor), *Medieval Art and Architecture at Exeter Cathedral* (Exeter, 1991), pp.10-18. (Updated version of a paper originally published in *British Archaeological Association Conference Transactions* 1985.)

Building Research Establishment, 'The Selection of Natural Building Stone', *BRE Digest* 269, Jan 1983.

Building Research Establishment, 'Decay and Conservation of Stone Masonry', *BRE Digest* 177, May 1975.

Richard Durman, 'Hamstone in Salisbury', *Sarum Chronicle* 1 (2001), pp. 29-36.

C. M. Gerrard, 'Ham Hill Stone: A medieval distribution pattern from Somerset', *Oxford Journal of Archaeology* 4(1) (1985), pp. 105-12.

G. W. Green, 'The Geology of Building Stone in Dorset, Hampshire and Wiltshire, together with some adjacent parts of Somerset', *The Hatcher Review* V:45 (1998), pp. 5-17.

Alison Henry, 'Hamstone: History, Use and Conservation' (unpublished dissertation, University of Bristol,1992).

Alison Henry, *Lime: A Guide to the Use of Lime in Historic Buildings* (Yeovil: Conservation & Environment Department, South Somerset District Council, 1999).

R. M. H. Lawrence, 'Ham Hill Stone' (unpublished dissertation, University of Bath, 2003).

Tim Palmer, 'Ham Hill Stone', *Natural Stone Specialist* (March 1997), pp.18-20.

Tim Tatton-Brown, 'The Building Stone for Salisbury Cathedral', *The Hatcher Review* V:45 (1998), pp. 39-47.

Jo Thomas, 'The Lesser-known Building Materials of West Dorset', *Proceedings of the Geologists' Association* 101 (1990), pp. 289-300.

Jo Thomas, 'The Building Stones of Dorset', Parts I – IV, *Proceedings of the Dorset Natural History & Archaeological Society* 114-17 (1992-95), pp. 61-70; 95-100; 133-8; 161-8 respectively.

Christopher Woodward, 'Stone', *Conservation Advisory Booklet No. 1* (The Building of Bath Museum and Bath City Council, 1994).

Index

Numbers in **bold** refer to captions of illustrations

237

241